SARA CREWE
The Little Princess

Frances Hodgson Burnett (1849 - 1924) was an English playwright and author, best known for her children's stories - in particular *Little Lord Fauntleroy* (1886), *A Little Princess* (1905), and *The Secret Garden* (1911).

Born near Manchester, England, her family emigrated to the USA in 1865, where she began writing to help earn money for the family. She is buried in Roslyn Cemetery, on Long Island, and a memorial sculpture - depicting her two famous Secret Garden characters, Mary and Dickon - was erected in her honour in Central Park's Conservatory Garden in 1936.

SARA CREWE
The Little Princess

Three-Act Playscript of the Classic Novel

Story by Frances Hodgson Burnett
Adapted for the Stage by Rachel Louise Lawrence

BlackdownPublications

This adaption of Frances Hodgson Burnett's 1902 play *"A Little Un-fairy Princess"* and 1905 novel *"A Little Princess"* first published in 2014 by Blackdown Publications

Copyright © 2014 Rachel Louise Lawrence

Rachel Louise Lawrence has asserted her right to be identified as the author of this work

Illustration on front cover by Harold H. Piffard (1867-1938)

ISBN-13: 978-1503282421
ISBN-10: 1503282422

CAUTION All rights whatsoever in this play are strictly reserved. Requests to reproduce the text in whole or in part should be addressed to the publisher.

PERFORMING RIGHTS Applications for performance, including readings and excerpts, in the English language throughout the world should be addressed to Performing Rights Manager at the following address

Blackdown*Publications*
Address 83 Blackdown View, Ilminster, Somerset TA19 0BD
Email blackdownpublications@mail.com

No performance of any kind may be given unless a license has been obtained. Applications should be made before rehearsals begin.

SARA CREWE

The Little Princess

SUMMARY

Sara Crewe, a parlour-boarder at Miss Minchin's Select Seminary for Young Ladies, is left in poverty when her father dies, but is later rescued by a mysterious benefactor

SETTING

London, 1902

ACT I	*Schoolroom, Miss Minchin's Seminary - Sara Crewe's 11th birthday party*
ACT II	
Scene I	*Garret, Miss Minchin's Seminary - a month later*
Scene II	*Garret, Miss Minchin's Seminary - several months later, winter*
ACT III	*Study, Residence of Mr Carrisford - the following morning*

CHARACTERS

Living at Miss Minchin's Seminary

SARA CREWE, *daughter of Captain Ralph Crewe, 11-years-old, English father, French mother (who died when born), but raised in India until the age of 7, she is intelligent, polite and creative*

MARIA MINCHIN, *proprietor and Headmistress of Seminary*

AMELIA MINCHIN, *younger sister of Miss Minchin, teacher at Seminary*

BECKY, *scullery maid, 14-years-old*

ERMENGARDE ST. JOHN, *Sara's best friend, 11-years-old, she is affectionate, slow and overweight*

LOTTIE LEGH, *Sara's adopted 'daughter', 6-years-old*

LAVINIA HERBERT, *nemesis of Sara Crewe, 14-years-old*

JESSIE, *Lavinia's best friend*

EMMA, *maid*

Other Parlour Boarders, LILLY, BLANCHE, GERTRUDE, *and* MARJORIE

Neighbours across the street from Miss Minchin's Seminary

MR CARMICHAEL, *personal lawyer for Mr Carrisford and father of the 'Large Family'*

MRS CARMICHAEL, *mother of the 'Large Family'*

JANET CARMICHAEL, *eldest daughter of the 'Large Family'*

NORA CARMICHAEL, *daughter of the 'Large Family'*

MAZIE CARMICHAEL, *daughter of the 'Large Family'*

DONALD CARMICHAEL, *son of the 'Large Family', 6-years-old*

Next-door neighbours to Miss Minchin's Seminary

TOM CARRISFORD, *childhood friend and business partner of Captain Crewe*

RAM DASS, *Lascar and manservant to Mr Carrisford*

JAMES, *secretary to Mr Carrisford*

Visitor to Miss Minchin's Seminary

MR BARROW, *Captain Crewe's lawyer of the firm 'Barrow & Skipworth'*

ACT I

A large schoolroom at "Miss Minchin's Select Seminary for Young Ladies"; central window with view of Snow Street; fireplace with fire lighted; and on the walls are four bracket-lamps and four maps. In front window a platform on which there is a blackboard easel. The room contains a table, a sofa above fireplace, a piano with bench behind it, and several chairs.

At the rise of curtain: JESSIE at piano; ERMENGARDE, LOTTIE, BLANCHE, LILLY, MARJORIE in ring; LAVINIA and GERTRUDE sitting; AMELIA upstage

JESSIE plays a waltz. GIRLS dance.

GIRLS - *(counting)* One, two, three, four ...

AMELIA - *(breaking in upon the noise)* Stop, stop, girls! Do stop. I only wanted to try the music before the company came.

   (GIRLS stop and get into lines)

Let me look at you all.

   (LAVINIA crossing)

Don't poke your head forward. Please turn out your toes.

   (LILLY has crossed to right)

Lilly, your sash is untied. Let me tie it for you. *(AMELIA does so)*

You know Miss Minchin.

LAVINIA - Huh!

AMELIA - I will be very angry if there is any rude or unladylike conduct this afternoon. The lady and gentleman who live across the street in number 46 are coming in to see you. They have a very large family - nearly all old enough to go to a genteel school. That's why dear Sara is giving you this party.

LAVINIA - 'Dear Sara'... huh!

AMELIA - Now, Lavinia, what do you mean by that?

LAVINIA - Oh, nothing, Miss Amelia.

ERMENGARDE - Oh, she did it because she's jealous of Sara.

LAVINIA - I didn't.

ERMENGARDE - You did.

LAVINIA - I didn't.

ERMENGARDE - Did.

LAVINIA - Didn't!

ERMENGARDE - Did.

AMELIA - *(coming between them)* Stop. I never saw such rude conduct.

(LAVINIA laughs)

You are a spiteful child, Lavinia. I believe you are jealous. It's very nice indeed of Sara to give you all this party on her birthday. It's not every child who cares about her schoolfellows. And she has not looked at one of her beautiful presents yet because she wanted you to have the pleasure of seeing them unpacked.

(GIRLS crowd around her)

GIRLS - Ah...! *(Dance around her)*

ERMENGARDE - Are they going to be unpacked here?

GIRLS - Yes, yes, yes!

LAVINIA - *(sarcastically)* Did her Papa send them all from India, Miss Amelia?

LILLY - Did he?

AMELIA - *(grandly)* Most of them came from Paris.

GIRLS - Oh...! Paris.

AMELIA - There is a doll that was ordered months ago.

GIRLS - Oh, a doll!

AMELIA - And a whole trunk full of things like a real young lady.

LOTTIE - *(jumping up and down)* Are we going to see them right this minute?

AMELIA - Miss Minchin said they might be brought in after you had tried the new waltz.

LOTTIE - Tra-la-la! *(dancing)*

AMELIA - I am going to tell her you have finished.

(laughter)

Now do be nice and quiet when I leave you.

(ERMENGARDE swings LOTTIE around)

Lottie, don't rumple your new sash. One of you big girls must look after her.

(LOTTIE picks up pillow from sofa, ready to throw at LAVINIA)

Now do be quiet. *(Exit)*

(As AMELIA exits, ERMENGARDE runs up to door. GIRLS, except

LAVINIA, *form picture on platform.)*

ERMENGARDE - It's all right, girls. She's gone.

(LOTTIE throws pillow at LAVINIA and runs around the room, with LAVINIA in pursuit. ERMENGARDE runs to LOTTIE'S rescue.)

LOTTIE - *(as LAVINIA catches her and drags her)* Ermie, Ermie. Oh! Oh!

(ERMENGARDE catches LOTTIE'S other hand and drags her away from LAVINIA; other GIRLS watch)

GIRLS - Now!

(JESSIE playing piano, GIRLS begin to do "ring around" again, laughing and chattering the while)

LAVINIA - I wish you girls wouldn't make so much noise. Jessie, stop playing that silly polka.

GIRLS - No, no, go on, Jessie, go on.

(LOTTIE runs over and pushes LAVINIA twice, falling the second time and hurting her knee)

LOTTIE - Oh! Ah! Oh!

LAVINIA - I never saw such rough things. I wish Miss Minchin would come in and catch you.

LOTTIE - I guess it's all right.

MARJORIE - We're not going to stop, just because you want to talk.

BLANCHE - You girls think you are so big. You always try to stop the fun. Jessie, go on.

(JESSIE at the piano, begins playing again)

ERMENGARDE - I'm going to be the leader.

(ERMENGARDE skips across room to piano and grabs the sheet music; JESSIE stops playing suddenly)

MARJORIE - What's the matter?

JESSIE - Oh, girls! Ermengarde has thrown all the music into the piano.

(GIRLS crowd around her and take the sheet music out of the piano - ERMENGARDE laughing)

LAVINIA - You'd stop fast enough if it was the Princess Sara talking.

ERMENGARDE - Oh, we all like Sara. *We're* not jealous of her.

(GIRLS exclamations of assent; JESSIE playing "London Bridge")

LAVINIA - Oh, of course you like Sara, just because she's the rich girl of the school and the show pupil. There's nothing so very grand in having a father who lives in India, even if he is in the army.

LOTTIE - At any rate he's killed tigers, and he sends Sara the most beautiful presents! *(Pulls LAVINIA'S hair)*

GERTRUDE - And he's told Miss Minchin that she can have anything she wants.

ERMENGARDE - She's cleverer than any of us. My father says he'd give thousands of pounds if I were as clever as she is. She actually likes to read books. I can't bear them.

LAVINIA - *(contemptuously)* We all know that.

ERMENGARDE - Well, if I am the stupidest girl in the school, Sara's the nicest. You don't see Sara walking with her friends and saying spiteful things.

(Bell rings off. GIRLS run into straight lines. ERMENGARDE to blackboard and draws a cat. LAVINIA moves to stand upstage by

the door.)

GIRLS - Miss Minchin's coming! Miss Minchin's coming!

LAVINIA - *(open door slightly)* Yes, and leading Sara by the hand as if she were a "Little Princess".

ERMENGARDE - *(pointing to board)* That old cat, Miss Minchin.

(GIRLS laugh. Enter MISS MINCHIN, leading SARA, is followed into room by EMMA and BECKY, who are carrying presents.)

MINCHIN - *(sweeping grandly down)* Silence, young ladies ... Emma, place yours on the table *(doll and nine books)*. Becky, place yours there *(trunk)*.

(BECKY looks at the GIRLS)

Becky, it is not your place to look at the young ladies. You forget yourself. *(waving EMMA and BECKY off)* Now you may leave us.

(EMMA exits. BECKY starts to follow her, but SARA places her hand on BECKY's elbow, stalling her progress out of the room.)

SARA - If you please, Miss Minchin, mayn't Becky stay?

MINCHIN - Becky! My dearest Sara!

SARA - I want her because I know she will like to see the presents. She is a little girl, too, you know.

MINCHIN - *(scandalised)* My dear Sara - Becky is the scullery maid. Scullery maids are not little girls - at least they ought not to be.

SARA - But Becky is, you know.

MINCHIN - I'm sorry to hear it.

SARA - I don't believe she can help it. And I know she would enjoy herself. *(crosses to MISS MINCHIN)* Please let her stay -

because it is my birthday.

(BECKY backs into the corner in mingled terror and delight)

MINCHIN - *(dignified)* Well ... as you ask it as a birthday favour - she may stay.

SARA - Thank you.

MINCHIN - Rebecca, thank Miss Sara for her great kindness.

BECKY - *(comes forward, making little charity curtseys, words tumbling over each other)* Oh, if you please, miss! Thank you, miss! I am that grateful, miss! I did want to see the doll, miss, that I did. I thank you, miss.

(SARA nods happily to BECKY, who bobs to MISS MINCHIN)

And thank you, ma'am, for letting me take the liberty.

MINCHIN - Go stand over there. *(pointing grandly to corner)* Not too near the young ladies.

(BECKY backs into corner, rolls down sleeves etc)

Now, young ladies, I have a few words to say to you. *(sweeping grandly up to platform)*

BLANCHE - *(aside)* She's going to make a speech. I wish it was over.

MINCHIN - You are aware, young ladies, that dear Sara is eleven years old today.

GIRLS - Yes, Miss Minchin.

LAVINIA - *(mutters)* 'Dear Sara!'

MINCHIN - Several of you here have also been eleven years old, but Sara's birthdays are rather different from other little girls' birthdays.

GIRLS - Yes, Miss Minchin.

MINCHIN - When she is older she will be heiress to a large fortune, which it will be her duty to spend in a meritorious manner.

ERMENGARDE - No, Miss Minchin - I mean yes, Miss Minchin.

MINCHIN - When her Papa, Captain Crewe, brought her from India and gave her into my care, he said to me, in a jesting manner, "I'm afraid she will be very rich, Miss Minchin."

GIRLS - Oh! - Ah! - Oh!

MINCHIN - My reply was, "Her education at my seminary, Captain Crewe, shall be such as will adorn the largest fortune."

(LOTTIE sniffs loudly)

Lottie, do not sniff. Use your pocket handkerchief.

(ERMENGARDE wipes LOTTIE'S nose. LOTTIE sniffs again.)

Sara has become my most accomplished pupil. Her French and her dancing are a credit to the seminary. Her manners - which have caused you all to call her Princess Sara - are perfect. Her amiability she exhibits by giving you this afternoon's party. I hope you appreciate her generosity. I wish you to express your appreciation by saying aloud, all together, "Thank you, Sara."

GIRLS - Thank you, Sara.

ERMENGARDE - *(alone)* Thank you, Sara.

BECKY - I thank you, miss.

SARA - I thank you for coming to my party. *(retires)*

MINCHIN - Very pretty indeed, Sara. That is what a real princess does when the populace applauds.

(LAVINIA scoffs behind her hand)

Lavinia *(scathingly)* the sound you just made was extremely like a snort. If you are jealous of your fellow pupil, I beg you will express your feelings in some more ladylike manner. I have one thing more to say. The visitors coming are the father and mother of a large family. I wish you to conduct yourselves in such a manner as will cause them to observe that elegance of deportment can be acquired at 'Miss Minchin's Seminary'.

(ERMENGARDE poses in corner)

I will now go back to the drawing room until they arrive and leave you to enjoy yourselves. Sara, you may show your presents. *(MISS MINCHIN exits)*

ERMENGARDE - *(imitates MISS MINCHIN'S walk)* 'Sara, you may show your presents!'

AMELIA - *(coming out from behind)* Ermengarde!

ERMENGARDE - Oh! Miss Amelia ...

(AMELIA crosses to door)

Please forgive me. I did - didn't -

(AMELIA exits. GIRLS laugh and flock around the boxes on table etc.)

SARA - *(getting chair from piano)* She caught you that time, Ermie. *(getting on chair behind table)* Which shall we look at first? *(picking up books)* These are books, I know. *(trying to untie them)*

GIRLS - *(disgusted)* Oh ... books ... oh.

ERMENGARDE - *(aghast)* Does your Papa send you books for a birthday present? Why, he's as bad as mine. Don't open them, Sara.

SARA - *(laughing)* But I like them the best - never mind though. This is the doll. *(uncovering long wooden box)* I'll open that first. *(stands doll upon its feet – doll is on a metal stand)*

GIRLS - Oh! - Ah! - Oh!

LILLY - Isn't she a beauty?

(BECKY gets stool from above door and stands on it to see doll)

BLANCHE - She's almost as big as Lottie.

LOTTIE - *(dancing down)* Tra-la-la

LILLY - She's dressed for the theatre. See her magnificent opera cloak.

(LAVINIA does not get on floor)

ERMENGARDE - She has an opera glass in her hand.

SARA - So she has. *(getting down)* Here's her trunk. Let us open that and look at her things; Ermie, you open the other.

(SARA takes trunk with JESSIE downstage and opens it. ERMENGARDE takes other one, with help of LILLY, and opens it too. GIRLS crowd around trunks, sit on floor, looking at the clothes. BECKY looks on from behind)

Here is the key.

GIRLS - Oh!

SARA - This is full of lace collars and silk stockings and handkerchiefs. Here's a jewel case with a necklace and a tiara of diamonds. Put them on her, Lilly. All of her underclothes. Ah, look. *(showing)*

ERMENGARDE - Here's a velvet coat trimmed with chinchilla, and one lined with ermine, and muffs. Oh, what darling dresses! A pale cloth, trimmed with sable, and a long coat.

(LOTTIE takes coat and puts it on)

A pink, covered with white little buttons, and a white tulle dress, and dresses, dresses, dresses!

SARA - And here are hats, and hats, and hats. Becky, can you see? *(rises)*

BECKY - Oh, yes, miss, and it's like 'eaven *(falls off stool backwards)*

SARA - *(rises)* She is a lovely doll. *(looking at doll)* Suppose she understands human talk, and feels proud of being admired.

LAVINIA - You are always *supposing* things, Sara.

SARA - I know I am. I like it. There's nothing so nice as supposing. It's almost like being a fairy. If you suppose anything hard enough, it seems as if it were real. Have you never done it?

LAVINIA - *(contemptuously)* No - of course not - it's ridiculous.

SARA - Is it?

LAVINIA - It's all very well to suppose things if you have everything. Could you suppose and pretend if you were a beggar and lived in a garret?

SARA - *(thoughtful)* I believe I could. If one was a beggar, one would have to suppose and pretend all the time. But it mightn't be easy.

(LAVINIA turns away)

Suppose we finish looking at the doll's things when we have more time. Becky will put them back in the trunk.

(LOTTIE goes up to doll, to see tiara.)

BECKY - *(comes forward quickly - shyly)* Me, miss? Yes, miss. Thank you, miss, for letting me touch them. *(down on knees, wiping hands)* Oh, my! They are beautiful.

LAVINIA - *(at table, catching LOTTIE touching doll)* Get down this minute. That's not for babies to touch. *(takes LOTTIE'S arm)*

LOTTIE - *(crying)* I'm not a baby!

JESSIE - There now, you've made her cry - the spoiled thing.

LAVINIA - Stop it this minute, you cry-baby! Stop this minute!

LOTTIE - I'm not a cry-baby! I'm not! Sa-ra, Sa-ra ... Oh!

SARA - *(runs to LOTTIE; kneeling)* Now. Lottie. Lottie, dear, you mustn't cry.

LOTTIE - *(howling)* I don't want to stay in a nasty school with nasty girls.

SARA - *(to LAVINIA and JESSIE)* You ought not to have scolded her. She's such a little thing. And you know she's only at boarding school because she hasn't any mother.

(GIRLS sympathetic; JESSIE to door)

LOTTIE - *(wailing)* I haven't any Mamma!

JESSIE - If she doesn't stop, Miss Minchin will hear her.

(ERMENGARDE takes tiara from doll)

LILLY - And she'll be so cross that she may stop the party. Do stop, darling Lottie. I'll give you a penny.

LOTTIE - Don't want your old penny.

ERMENGARDE - Yes, do stop, and I'll give you anything *(offering box)*

SARA - Now, Lottie, you promised Sara."

LOTTIE - She called me a cry-baby *(crying)*

SARA - *(petting her)* But if you cry, you will be one, Lottie pet. You promised. There, there.

LOTTIE - I haven't any Mamma.

SARA - *(cheerfully)* Yes, you have, darling. Have you forgotten? Don't you remember we said that Sara is your Mamma? Don't you want Sara to be your Mamma?

(LOTTIE stops crying)

See. *(rising and giving doll to LOTTIE)* I'll lend you my doll to hold while I tell you that story I promised you.

GERTRUDE - Oh, do tell us a story, Sara. *(puts doll on chair)*

JESSIE - Oh, yes, do.

GIRLS - Oh!

SARA - I may not have time to finish it before the company comes - but I'll tell you the end some other time.

(LOTTIE takes doll to chair)

LAVINIA - That's always the way, Princess Sara. *(passionately)* Nasty little spoilt beast. I should like to *slap* her.

SARA - *(firing up)* I should like to slap you too. But I don't want to slap you! At least I both *want* to slap you and should *like* to slap you.

GIRLS - *(in group, interested in fight)* Oh, oh!

SARA - But I won't slap you. We are not little gutter girls. We are old enough to know better.

LAVINIA - Ah, yes ... Your Royal Highness. We are princesses, I believe - or at least one of us is - Jessie told me you often pretended to yourself that you were a princess. The school ought to be very fashionable now Miss Minchin has a princess for a pupil.

SARA - *(getting control of herself)* It's true. Sometimes I do pretend I'm a princess. I pretend I am a princess so that I can try to behave like one.

GIRLS - Ah!

LAVINIA - Dear me, I hope, when you ascend the throne, you won't forget us!

SARA - I won't.

(SARA stands still and stares at LAVINIA steadily as she takes JESSIE'S arm and turns away)

ERMENGARDE - You are queer, Sara, but you're nice. *(hugs her)*

SARA - I know I'm queer, and I try to be nice. Shall I begin the story?

GIRLS - *(ad lib.)* Story. Oh, oh! Yes, yes, begin, Sara, do.

SARA - I'm going to turn all the lights out. It's always so much nicer to tell a story by firelight. *(turns out brackets with switch above fireplace; gets on sofa for story)*

(All the GIRLS sit on the floor in front of the sofa, except LAVINIA, who stands near the piano)

LILLY - It's such fun to sit in the dark.

SARA - Once upon a time - long ago - there lived on the edge of a deep, deep forest a little girl and her grandmother.

GERTRUDE - Was she pretty?

SARA - She was so fair and sweet that people called her Snowflower. She had no relations in the world but her old grandmother, Dame Frosty-face.

JESSIE - Was she a nice old woman?

SARA - She was always nice to Snowflower. They lived together in a little cottage thatched with reeds. Tall trees sheltered it, daisies grew thick about the door, and swallows built in the eaves.

LILLY - What a nice place!

SARA - One sunny morning Dame Frosty-face said, "My child. I am going a long journey, and I cannot take you with me, and I will tell you what to do when you feel lonely. You know that carved oak chair I sit in by the fire. Well, lay your head on the velvet cushions and say, 'Chair of my Grandmother, tell me a story', and it will tell you one."

GIRLS - Oh!

SARA - "And if you want to travel anywhere, just seat yourself in it, and say, 'Chair of my Grandmother, take me where I want to go.'"

ERMENGARDE - Oh, I wish I had a chair like that.

BLANCHE - Oh, go on, Sara.

GIRLS - Yes, do go on.

ERMENGARDE - And so ...

LOTTIE - And so ...

SARA - And so Dame Frosty-face went away. And every day Snowflower baked herself a barley cake, and every night the chair told her a beautiful new story.

ERMENGARDE - If it had been my chair, I should have told it to take me to the King's palace.

SARA - That is what happened - but listen. The time passed on, but Dame Frosty-face did not come back for such a long time that Snowflower thought she would go and find her.

MARJORIE - Did she find her?

SARA - Wait and listen. One day she jumped into the chair and said, "Chair of my Grandmother, take me the way she went."

And the chair gave a creak and began to move out of the cottage and into the forest where all the birds were singing.

ERMENGARDE - How I wish I could have gone with her.

SARA - And the chair went on, and on, and on - like a coach and six.

LOTTIE - How far did it go?

SARA - It travelled through the forest and through the ferns, and over the velvet moss - it travelled one day, and two days, and three days - and on the fourth day -

LILLY - What did it do?

SARA - *(slowly)* It came to an open place in the forest where a hundred workmen were felling trees and a hundred wagons were carrying them away to the King's palace.

ERMENGARDE - Was the King giving a ball?

SARA - He was giving seven of them. Seven days of feasting to celebrate the birthday of his daughter, the Princess Greedalend.

BLANCHE - Did he invite Snowflower?

SARA - Listen. The chair marched up to the palace, and all the people ran after it. And the King heard of it, and the Lords and Ladies crowded to see it, and when the Princess heard it was a chair that could tell stories she cried until the King sent an order to the little girl to come and make it tell her one.

LOTTIE - Did she go in?

LILLY - Oh, how lovely!

SARA - The chair marched in a grave and courtly manner up the grand staircase and into the palace hall. The King sat on an ivory throne in a robe of purple velvet, stiff with flowers of gold. The Queen sat on his right hand in a mantle clasped with pearls, and the Princess wore a robe of gold sewn with diamonds.

LILLY - Oh, what splendid clothes!

SARA - But Snowflower had little bare feet, and nothing but a clean, coarse linen dress. She got off the chair and made a curtsey to the grand company. Then she laid her head on the cushion, and said, "Chair of my Grandmother, tell me a story" and a clear, silvery voice came out from the old velvet cushion, and said, "Listen to the story of the Christmas cuckoo."

(Doorbell peals)

ALL GIRLS - *(jumping up from floor and sofa, forming two lines, in readiness for the visitors)* Miss Minchin is coming! Miss Minchin is coming!

(Enter MISS MINCHIN, followed by AMELIA; BECKY under the table)

MINCHIN - What are you naughty girls doing in the dark? Amelia, turn up the lights immediately.

(AMELIA does so with switch above fireplace)

How dare you?

SARA - I beg pardon, Miss Minchin. It was my entire fault. I was telling them a story, and I like to tell them in the firelight.

MINCHIN - *(changing)* Oh, it was you, Sara. That is a different matter. I can always trust you.

LAVINIA - *(aside)* Yes, of course, if it's the Princess Sara, it's a different matter.

MINCHIN - *(speaking off to MRS CARMICHAEL)* Won't you come in, Mrs Carmichael?

(Enter MRS CARMICHAEL, followed by DONALD, MAZIE, NORA and JANET in a line. DONALD has his mother's shirt in his hand, playing horse; three girls are dressed for the street. They follow MRS CARMICHAEL to sofa and sit down.)

MINCHIN - She *(referring to SARA)* is such a clever child. Such an imagination. She amuses the girls by the hour with her wonderful storytelling.

MRS CARMICHAEL - She has a clever little face.

(ERMENGARDE offers to make friends with DONALD, who fights her into corner)

MINCHIN - Won't you sit here, Mrs Carmichael? *(indicating sofa)*

MRS CARMICHAEL - I hope I won't disturb the dancing if I am obliged to leave you suddenly.

MINCHIN - You will not disturb us, although we shall, of course, be very sorry.

MRS CARMICHAEL - Mr Carmichael has just had bad news from an important client in India. The poor man has suddenly lost all his money and is on his way to England, very ill indeed.

MINCHIN - How distressing!

MRS CARMICHAEL - Mr Carmichael may be called away at any moment. He said he would send a servant for me if he received a summons to go. If it comes I shall be obliged to run away at once. The children wanted so much to see the dancing that I did not like to disappoint them.

MINCHIN - Sara, my dear, come here. *(aside to MRS CARMICHAEL)* Her mother died when she was born. Her father is a most distinguished young officer - very rich, fortunately. *(to SARA)* Shake hands with Mrs Carmichael.

(SARA does so)

(to MRS CARMICHAEL) Sara is eleven years old today, Mrs Carmichael, and is giving a party to her schoolfellows. She is always doing things to give her friends pleasure.

MRS CARMICHAEL - *(motherly woman, pats SARA'S hand)* She looks like a kind little girl.

(LOTTIE brings doll over to sofa and shows it to the CARMICHAEL GIRLS)

I'm sure my children would like to hear her tell stories. They love stories, and some day you must come and tell them one. *(turns and sees doll)* Oh, what a splendid doll! Is it yours?

MINCHIN - *(grandly)* Her Papa ordered it in Paris. Its wardrobe was made by a fashionable dressmaker. Nothing is too superb for the child.

LOTTIE - *(to SARA)* Sara, may that little boy hold your doll?

SARA - Yes, dear.

(LOTTIE takes doll to DONALD, who boxes it away from him, boy fashion)

LOTTIE - *(taking doll out of harms way)* He's one of the large family across the street - the ones you make up stories about.

MRS CARMICHAEL - *(good-naturedly)* Do you make up stories about us?

SARA - I hope you won't mind. I can see your house out of my window, and there are so many of you, and you all look so happy together, that I like to pretend I know you all. I suppose things about you.

(CARMICHAEL GIRLS have been standing in two lines listening to all this)

LILLY - She has made up names for all of you.

MRS CARMICHAEL - Has she? What are they?

SARA - They are only pretended names - perhaps you'll think they're silly.

MRS CARMICHAEL - No, I shall not. What do you call us?

LOTTIE - *(solemnly)* You are Mrs and Mr Montmorency.

MRS CARMICHAEL - *(laughing)* What a grand name! And what do you call the children?

SARA - *(shy but smiling)* The little boy in the lace cap is Ethelbert Beaucham Montmorency - and the second baby is Violette Cholmondeley Montmorency, and the little boy with the fat brown legs and socks is Sidney Cecil Vivienne Montmorency.

LOTTIE - *(interrupting and dancing)* Then there's Lillian Evangeline - and Guy Clarence - and Maude - Marion - and Veronia Eustacia - and Claude Audrey Harold Hector. *(laughs and goes into corner)*

MRS CARMICHAEL - You romantic little thing!

SARA - *(apologetically)* I shouldn't have supposed so much about you if you hadn't all looked so happy together. My Papa is a soldier in India, you know, and my Mamma died when I was a baby. So I like to look at children who have Mammas and Papas.

MRS CARMICHAEL - *(kissing SARA)* You poor little dear - Miss Minchin must let you come and have tea with us.

MINCHIN - Certainly, certainly. Sara will be delighted. Now, young ladies, you may begin the entertainment Sara has prepared for Mrs Carmichael.

(Enter EMMA)

EMMA - A gentleman would like to see you, ma'am. He says he comes from Messrs. Barrow & Skipworth.

MINCHIN - The lawyers? *(annoyed)* What can he want? I cannot be disturbed at present. Ask him to wait.

EMMA - And if you please, ma'am, a note for Mrs Carmichael.

(Delivers same to MRS CARMICHAEL, who rises to receive it, and goes downstage. Exit EMMA.)

MRS CARMICHAEL - A note for me? *(takes it and opens note)*

MINCHIN - Not bad news, I hope?

MRS CARMICHAEL - Very bad, I am afraid. My husband's client, poor Mr Carrisford, has just landed, dangerously ill. Much worse. Mr Carmichael wants me to go and see him at once. I am so sorry to run away like this. It has all been so charming. Thank you for asking us. Come, girls. Say good afternoon. Papa needs us. *(shaking hands with MISS MINCHIN)* Your school is delightful.

(Exit MRS CARMICHAEL and GIRLS in same order as entrance, DONALD driving his mother as before)

DONALD - Giddyap - whoa - go along.

GIRLS - Goodbye. Good afternoon, etc.

AMELIA - What a pity she was obliged to leave so soon.

MINCHIN - She was evidently very much pleased.

EMMA - *(entering)* Will you see the gentleman from Messrs. Barrow & Skipworth, ma'am?

AMELIA - *(meekly)* The girls' refreshments are laid in your parlour, sister. Could you see him in here while the girls have their cake and sherry?

MINCHIN - Yes. *(to GIRLS)* Now, young ladies, you must go and enjoy the nice things Sara has for you.

(GIRLS all troop out)

GIRLS - Cake and sherry.

MINCHIN - *(to EMMA)* Bring the gentleman in here.

(Exit EMMA. Enter MR BARROW, ushered on by EMMA. MR BARROW is a middle-aged, high-class lawyer, well-dressed.)

EMMA - Mr Barrow, ma'am. *(exit EMMA)*

MINCHIN - Good evening, sir. Pray, be seated. *(indicating sofa)* Of the legal firm of Barrow & Skipworth, I believe?

BARROW - Yes, Miss Minchin.

(MR BARROW does not sit down at once, his attention attracted by the presents)

A hundred pounds. All expensive material and made at a Parisian modiste's. He spent money lavishly enough, that young man.

MINCHIN - *(stiffly)* I beg your pardon, Mr. Barrow. I do not understand.

BARROW - Birthday presents to a child eleven years old! Mad extravagance, I call it.

MINCHIN - Captain Crewe is a man of fortune. The diamond mines alone -

BARROW - Diamond mines! There are none! Never were!

MINCHIN - *(startled, stands)* What! What do you mean?

BARROW - At any rate, it would have been much better if there never had been any. Miss Minchin, I represent the late Captain Crewe -

MLNCHIN - *(startled)* The late Captain Crewe? The late! You don't mean to say that Captain Crewe -

BARROW - *(sits on sofa)* He's dead, ma'am. Died of jungle fever.

MINCHIN - *(shocked)* It seems impossible. How shocking! How sudden!

BARROW - It was sudden. The firm thought that you should be told at once, as his child is in your care.

MINCHIN - Very right and proper. Poor Captain Crewe! Poor little orphaned Sara. *(handkerchief to her eyes)* She will need my care more than ever.

BARROW - She will indeed, ma'am.

MINCHIN - What do you mean?

BARROW - That, as she hasn't a relation in the world that we know of to take charge of her, she is fortunate in having such a friend as yourself.

MINCHIN - Most certainly. An heiress to so large a fortune - for I believe it is a very large fortune?

(MR BARROW clears throat significantly. MISS MINCHIN takes him up sharply)

What do you mean? You certainly mean something. What is it?

BARROW - She has no fortune, ma'am, large or small. She is left without a penny.

MINCHIN - Without a penny! It's impossible. Captain Crewe was a rich man.

BARROW - Ah! Was - that's it, ma'am, he was.

MINCHIN - *(leaning forward excitedly)* You don't mean he has lost his money? Lost it?

BARROW - Every penny of it. That young man had too much money. He didn't know what to do with it, so he let a speculating friend - a very dear friend *(sarcastically)* - play ducks and drakes with it. The friend was mad on the subject of a high diamond mine - put all of his own money into it - all of Captain Crewe's - the mine proved a failure - the dear friend - the very dear friend - ran away. Captain Crewe was already stricken with fever when the news came - the shock was too much for him. He died delirious. *(rises)* Ruined.

MINCHIN - Do you mean to tell me that he has left nothing? That Sara will have no fortune! That the child is a beggar! That she is left on my hands a little pauper instead of an heiress?

BARROW - She is certainly left a beggar - and she is certainly left on your hands, ma'am.

MINCHIN - *(rising)* It's monstrous. She's in my drawing room, at this moment, dressed in a pink silk gown and lace petticoats, giving a party at my expense.

BARROW - She's certainly giving it at your expense, ma'am, if she's giving it. Barrow & Skipworth are not responsible for anything. There never was a cleaner sweep made of a man's fortune. Captain Crewe died without paying our last bill, and it was a considerable one.

MINCHIN - That is what has happened to me! I was always so sure of his payments that I went to all sorts of ridiculous expenses for the child. I paid the bills for that ridiculous doll and her ridiculous fantastic wardrobe. The child was to have anything she wanted. She has a carriage and a pony and a maid, and I've paid for all of them since the last cheque came.

BARROW - You hadn't better pay for anything more, ma'am, unless you want to make presents to the young lady. No one will remember you. She has not a brass farthing to call her own.

MINCHIN - But what am I to do? What am I to do?

BARROW - There isn't anything to do, ma'am. Captain Crewe is dead. The child is left a pauper. Nobody is responsible for her but you.

MINCHIN - I'm not responsible for her and I refuse to be made responsible for her!

BARROW - I have nothing to do with that, ma'am. I only know that Barrow & Skipworth are not responsible. Very sorry the thing has happened, of course. *(bows and turns to go)*

MINCHIN - If you think you can foist her off on me, you are greatly mistaken. I won't have it! I have been robbed, cheated! I will turn her out onto the streets!

BARROW - *(impersonally)* I wouldn't, ma'am, if I were you - it wouldn't look well. Ugly story to get about in connection with your establishment - pupil bundled out penniless and without friends. Pay you better to keep her as a sort of charity pupil.

MINCHIN - This is infamous. I'll do nothing of the sort.

BARROW - She's a clever child, I believe. She might teach the little ones, run errands, and that sort of thing - you can get a good deal out of her as she grows older.

MINCHIN - I will get a good deal out of her before she grows older!

BARROW - Just as you please, ma'am. The matter is entirely in your hands. Good afternoon. Very sorry the thing has happened, of course. Unpleasant for all parties. Good afternoon. *(exit)*

GIRLS - *(singing offstage)* "Here we go round the mulberry bush, the mulberry bush, the mulberry bush, - here we go round the mulberry bush, so early in the morning."

(MISS MINCHIN stands a moment, glaring after MR BARROW, then she starts toward door but stops as AMELIA enters.)

AMELIA - What's the matter, sister?

MINCHIN - *(fiercely and hoarsely)* Where is Sara Crewe?

AMELIA - *(astonished)* Sara? Why, she's with the girls in your room.

MINCHIN - Has she a black frock in her sumptuous wardrobe?

AMELIA - A black frock? A black one?

MINCHIN - She has frocks of every other colour. Has she a black one?

AMELIA - *(stammering)* Why - what - no - yes! But it is too short for her. She has only an old black velvet and she has outgrown it."

MINCHIN - Go tell her to take off that preposterous pink silk gown, and put the black one on, whether it is too short or not. She is done with finery!

AMELIA - *(wringing hands)* Oh, sister! What can have happened?

MINCHIN - Captain Crewe is dead.

AMELIA - Oh!

MINCHIN - He died without a penny.

AMELIA - Oh!

MINCHIN - That spoilt, pampered, fanciful child is left a pauper on my hands.

AMELIA - Oh! *(sits on nearest chair)* Oh!

MINCHIN - Hundreds of pounds have I spent on nonsense for

her - hundreds of pounds! - and I shall never see a penny of it.

GIRLS - *(outside)* Ha, ha, ha! *(applause)*

MINCHIN - Go, put a stop to that ridiculous party of hers. Go and make her change her frock.

AMELIA - *(gapes and stares)* I? M-must I go and tell her now?

MINCHIN - *(fiercely)* This moment! Don't sit there staring like a goose. Go!

(Exit AMELIA)

GIRLS - *(singing)* "Here we go round the mulberry bush"

MINCHIN - Hundreds of pounds! I never hesitated at the cost of anything. Princess Sara, indeed! The child has been pampered as if she had been a queen.

(loud sniffles from BECKY under table)

What is that? How dare you! How dare you! Come out immediately!

BECKY - *(coming from under table)* If you please, 'm - it's me, mum. *(sobs)* I know I hadn't ought to, but I was lookin' at the doll, mum - an' I was frightened when you come in - an' slipped under the table.

MINCHIN - You have been there all the time, listening.

BECKY - No, mum, not listenin'. *(bobbing curtsy)* I thought I could slip out without your noticin', but I couldn't an' I had to stay. But I didn't listen, mum--I wouldn't for nothin'. But I couldn't help hearin'."

MINCHIN - You impudent child!

BECKY - *(sobs frequently)* Oh, please 'm. I daresay you'll give me warnin', mum, but I'm so sorry for poor Miss Sara. She is such a kind young lady, mum.

MINCHIN - Leave the room.

BECKY - Yes, 'm. I will, 'm. But, oh, I just wanted to arst you - Miss Sara, she's been such a rich young lady, an' she's been waited on 'and and foot, an' what will she do now, mum, without no maid? If-if, oh please, would you let me wait on her after I've done my pots an' kettles? I'd do 'em that quick - if you'd let me wait on her now she's poor. Oh, poor little Miss Sara, mum - that was called a princess.

MINCHIN - *(even angrier)* No, certainly not. She'll wait on herself and on other people too. *(stamping foot)* Leave the room this instant - or you will leave this place.

BECKY - *(at door, turns)* Wouldn't you?

MINCHIN - Go!

(Exit BECKY)

(fiercely) Wait on her! No, she will not be waited on.

(Enter SARA with doll in arms, in black dress)

Come here.

(SARA advances a little)

Put down that doll. What do you mean by bringing her here? You will have no time for dolls in future.

SARA - No, I will not put her down. She is all I have. She was the last thing my Papa gave me before he died.

MINCHIN - He did not pay for her, at any rate. I paid for her.

SARA - *(crossing to chair and putting doll on it)* Then she is your doll, not mine.

MINCHIN - Of course she is my doll. *(crossing to table)* Everything that you have is mine. For a whole year I've been spending money on all sorts of ridiculously extravagant things for you, and I shall never be paid for one of them. I've been robbed, robbed, robbed!

SARA - *(turning from doll, suddenly and strongly)* My Papa did not mean to rob you. He did not. He did not!

MINCHIN - Whether he meant to do it or not, he did it - and here I am left with you on my hands. Do you understand?

SARA - Yes, I understand - Miss Amelia explained matters to me. *(kneels, covering face with arms, in doll's lap)* My Papa is dead! He left me no money. I am quite poor.

MINCHIN - You are a beggar. It appears that you have no relations and no home, and no one to take care of you.

(SARA does not respond)

What are you staring at? Are you so stupid that you cannot understand? I tell you that you are quite alone in the world. Remember that. You have no friends. You have no money. and have no one to do anything for you, unless I choose to keep you here out of charity.

SARA - *(quite yet proud)* I understand. I understand.

MINCHIN - Do not put on grand airs. The time for that sort of thing is past. You are not a princess any longer. Your pony and carriage will be sold at once. Your maid will be sent away. You'll wear your plainest and oldest frocks. Your extravagant ones are no longer suited for your station. You're like Becky - you will have to work for your living.

SARA - If you tell me what to do, I'll do it.

MINCHIN - You will be obliged to do it whether you like it or not. If I do not choose to keep you out of charity, you have no home but the street.

SARA - *(sobbing)* I know that.

MINCHIN - Then listen to what I say. If you work hard, and try to make yourself useful, I may let you stay here. You are a sharp child, and pick up things readily. You speak French very well, and you can help with the younger girls.

SARA - Yes, I can help with the little ones. I like them and they like me.

MINCHIN - Don't talk nonsense about people liking you. You are not a parlour-boarder now. You have to earn your bread. You will have more to do than to teach the little ones. You will run errands and help in the kitchen as well as in the schoolroom. If you don't please me you will be sent away. Remember that. Now go.

(SARA crosses to door to go)

Stop! Don't you intend to thank me?

SARA - What for?

MINCHIN - For my kindness to you - for my kindness in giving you a home.

SARA - *(fiercely)* You are not kind. You are not kind and it is not a home!

MINCHIN - Leave the room instantly.

(SARA starts to go)

Stop.

(SARA stops)

You are not to go to the bedroom you used to sleep in.

SARA - Where must I go?

MINCHIN - In future you will occupy the garret next to Becky's - under the roof.

SARA - The garret, next to Becky's? Where the rats are?

MINCHIN - Rubbish! There are no rats there. *(crossing to door)*

SARA - *(following to chair)* There are. Oh, Miss Minchin, there are! Sometimes Becky can hardly sleep at all. She says that in the garret next to hers they run about all night.

MINCHIN - Whether there are rats or not, you will sleep there. Leave the room. *(exit MISS MINCHIN)*

LOTTIE - *(outside)* Sara!

(Door opens, LOTTIE enters)

LOTTIE - Sara!

(LOTTIE embraces SARA, who is on her knees)

The big girls say your Papa is dead, like my Mamma; they say you haven't any Papa. Haven't you any Papa?

SARA - No, I haven't, Lottie - no, I haven't.

LOTTIE - You said you'd be my Mamma. I'll be your Papa, Sara. Let Lottie be your Papa.

SARA - Oh, Lottie, love me - please, Lottie, love me - love me.

Curtain

END OF ACT I

ACT II

Scene I

A garret under the roof at Miss Minchin's Seminary; rake roof with garret window, outside of which are showing housetops with snow on them. There are rat holes around; a bed, covered with old blanket, sheet, and old coverlet, badly torn; a table with bench behind it; chairs, an armchair, and a four-legged stool above fireplace; a washstand with pitcher, bowl, soap dish, and mug; an old trunk; and a candle in stick, unlighted.

SARA, wearing an old black frock, stands upon an old table and looking out of a window; enter LOTTIE

LOTTIE - *(aghast)* Sara! Mamma Sara!

(SARA turns, horrified, and jumps down from the table and runs to LOTTIE)

SARA - *(imploringly)* Don't cry and make a noise. I shall be scolded if you do, and I have been scolded all day.

LOTTIE - Are you very poor now, Sara? Are you as poor as a beggar? Is that why you live here? I don't want you to be as poor as a beggar.

SARA - Beggars have nowhere to live. I have a place to live in and it's-it's not such a bad room, Lottie.

LOTTIE - Isn't it? Why isn't it, Sara?

SARA - *(hugs LOTTIE close)* You can see all sorts of things you cannot see downstairs.

LOTTIE - What sort of things?

SARA - Chimneys - quite close to us - with smoke curling up in wreaths and clouds and going up into the sky. And sparrows hopping about and talking to each other, just as if they were people. And other garret windows where heads may pop out any minute and you can wonder who they belong to. And it all feels as high up - as if it was another world.

LOTTIE - Oh, let me see it! Lift me up!

SARA - *(lifts LOTTIE up to the table then stands next to her)* I wish someone lived next door. It is so close that if there was a little girl in the garret, we could talk to each other through the windows and climb over to see each other, if we were not afraid of falling.

LOTTIE - Oh, Sara! I like this garret - I like it! It is nicer than downstairs!

SARA - It is so little and so high above everything, that it is almost like a nest in a tree; and when the morning begins to come I can lie in bed and look right up into the sky through that flat window in the roof. It is like a square patch of light. If the sun is going to shine, little pink clouds float about, and I feel as if I could touch them. And if it rains, the drops patter and patter as if they were saying something nice. Then if there are stars, you can lie and try to count how many go into the patch. It takes such a lot. And just look at that tiny, rusty grate in the corner. If it was polished and there was a fire in it, just think how nice it would be. You see, it's really a beautiful little room.

SARA - *(holding LOTTIE'S hand, walking about the room)* You see, there could be a thick, soft blue Indian rug on the floor; and in that corner there could be a soft little sofa, with cushions to curl up on; and just over it could be a shelf full of books so that one could reach them easily; and there could be a fur rug before the fire, and hangings on the wall to cover up the whitewash, and pictures. They would have to be little ones, but they could be beautiful; and there could be a lamp with a deep rose-colored shade; and a table in the middle, with things to have tea with; and a little fat copper kettle singing on the hob; and the bed could be quite different. It could be made soft and covered with a lovely silk coverlet. It could be beautiful.

LOTTIE - Oh, Sara! I should like to live here!

SARA - Come, now, we must take you back downstairs before someone notices where you have gone to.

(Reluctantly, LOTTIE exits the garret room with SARA; moments pass, then SARA enters garret)

SARA - *(looking about her becomes desolate)* Oh, Lottie! It is a lonely place. Sometimes it is the loneliest place in the world.

(Cautious knock outside. Door is opened by ERMENGARDE, who at first looks around edge cautiously before entering.)

ERMENGARDE - Sara!

SARA - *(startled)* Ermengarde! What are you doing here? You will get into trouble.

ERMENGARDE - I know I shall, if I'm found out. But I don't care if I'm found out. I don't care a bit. Oh, Sara, please tell me. What is the matter? Why don't you like me anymore?

SARA - I do like you. I thought - you see, everything is different now - and I thought you were different.

ERMENGARDE - Why, it was you who were different! You didn't want to talk to me. I didn't know what to do. It was you who were different after I came back.

SARA - I am different, though not in the way you think. Miss Minchin does not want me to talk to the girls. Most of them don't want to talk to me. I thought - perhaps - you didn't. So I tried to keep out of your way.

ERMENGARDE - *(dismayed)* Oh, Sara. I couldn't bear it anymore. I dare say you could live without me, Sara, but I couldn't live without you. I was nearly dead. So tonight, when I was crying under the bedclothes, I thought all at once of creeping up here and just begging you to let us be friends again.

SARA - You are nicer than I am. I was too proud to try and make friends. You see, now that trials have come, they have shown that I am not a nice child. I was afraid they would. Perhaps that is what they were sent for.

ERMENGARDE - I don't see any good in them.

SARA - Neither do I, to speak the truth. But I suppose there might be good in things, even if we don't see it. *(doubtfully)* There might be good in Miss Minchin.

ERMENGARDE - Sara, how can bear living here?

SARA - I pretend it's quite different. I pretend it is a place in a story. Other people have lived in worse places. Think of the Count of Monte Cristo in the dungeons of the *Chateau d'If*. And think of the people in the Bastille!

ERMENGARDE - The Bastille ...

SARA - Yes - that is a good place to pretend about. I am a prisoner in the Bastille. I have been here for years and years and years, and everybody has forgotten about me. Miss

Minchin is the jailer and Becky is the prisoner in the next cell - I've told her about it - and I knock on the wall to make her hear, and she knocks like this *(knocks three times on wall; listens a moment)*. She's not there; if she were, she'd knock back. Ah!

ERMENGARDE - Will you tell me all about it? May I creep up here at night, whenever it is safe, and hear the things you have made up in the day? It will seem as if we were more 'best friends' than ever.

SARA - Yes. Adversity tries people, and mine has tried you and proved how nice you are.

Blackout

ACT II

Scene II

Months later, wind offstage; window opens and snow flutters through. Stage in semi-darkness. Broken pane in window.

Enter RAM DASS, appearing on platform back of window, with dark lantern. He raises window, examines room from platform with light, then beckons JAMES to follow him. Enter JAMES on platform, also carrying lantern.

JAMES - *(kneeling beside RAM DASS)* You saw the child go out?

RAM DASS - Yes, *Sahib*.

    (JAMES lets himself down by table through window)

JAMES - And no one ever enters here, but herself? You are sure?

RAM DASS - Sure, *Sahib*.

JAMES - Then we are safe for a few moments. We must look about and plan quickly. You have sharp ears; stand near the door. If we hear a sound on the stairs, we must bolt through the window.

RAM DASS - *(going to door)* Yes, *Sahib*. *(stands listening)*

JAMES - What a place to keep a child in! Was that a rat?

RAM DASS - Yes, a rat, *Sahib*. There are many in the walls.

JAMES - Ugh! It is a wonder the child is not terrified of them.

RAM DASS - The child is the little friend of all things, *Sahib*. She is not as other children. I see her when she does not see me. I slip across the slates and look at her many nights to see that she is safe. I watch her from my window when she does not know I am near. She stands on the table there and looks out at the sky as if it spoke to her. The rat she has fed and tamed in her loneliness. The poor slave of the house comes to her for comfort. There is a little child who comes to her in secret, there is one older who worships her and would listen to her forever if she might. This I have seen when I have crept across the roof. By the mistress of the house, she is treated like a pariah, but she has the bearing of a child who is of the blood of kings!

JAMES - You seem to know a great deal about her.

RAM DASS - Since *Sahib* returned to England, all her life, each day, I know. Her going out I know, and her coming in; her sadness and her poor joys; her coldness and her hunger. I know when she is alone until midnight, learning from her books; I know when her secret friends steal to her and she is happier - as children can be, even in the midst of poverty - because they come and she may laugh and talk with them in whispers. If she were ill, I should know, and I would come and serve her if it might be done.

JAMES - *(crossing to bed, making notes)* As hard as a stone. Coverlet dingy and worn, blanket thin, sheets patched and ragged. What a bed for a child to sleep in - and in a house which calls itself respectable! *(going to fire)* There has not been a fire in that grate for many a day.

RAM DASS - Never since I have seen it. The mistress of the house is not one who remembers that another than herself may be cold.

JAMES - We must alter this.

RAM DASS - *(at door)* When first my master thought of this plan, it made him smile, and he has not smiled for many days. He said, "The poor child will think a magician has worked a spell."

JAMES - *(back of table,)* She will indeed. It's a curious plan, but Mr Carrisford is a sick man and lonely. Now listen, Ram Dass. You Lascars can be as silent as ghosts. Can you steal in through that window and do what Mr Carrisford wishes, making no sound?

RAM DASS - Yes, Ram Dass can do it. He knows well how to make no sound at all.

JAMES - Will it be safer to do it while she is out upon some errand or at night when she is asleep?

RAM DASS - At night, when she sleeps. Girls sleep soundly, even the unhappy ones. I could have entered this room in the night many times, and without causing her to turn upon her pillow. If the other bearer passes to me the things through the window, I can do all and she will not stir. When she awakens she will think a magician has been here

JAMES - As Mr Carrisford's house is next door, you and I can bring the things across the roof together. Yes, yes, the window is wide enough to allow them to be passed through.

RAM DASS - Shall it be done tonight?

JAMES - Yes. Everything is ready - the measurements are correct. What's that?

RAM DASS - *(at door)* On the staircase two flights below. It is another child.

JAMES - Here - through here - quickly. *(exit through window)*

RAM DASS - *(in window)* Yes, Ram Dass will do this thing tonight. *(exit)*

(Enter SARA, shabbily dressed, wet, and tired; she closes door and stands a second leaning against it; looks about the room, out of breath and exhausted with climbing up stairs.)

SARA - I thought I should never get back, never, never. *(to table, lights candle)* How miserable it looks and how tired I am. *(takes hat and shawl and puts them on chair)* They are as wet as though they'd fallen in a pond. *(coming down to armchair, sits)* I've been sent out on errands ten times since breakfast. I'm cold - I'm wet - I'm as hungry as a wolf.

(Wind. Rats squeak. SARA has dropped head in lap on square stool. Hears rats, looks up.

Wind howls during this pause)

What a noise my rats are making - they must have heard me come in.

(First rat runs on)

Oh, there's Melchisedek. Poor thing, he's come to ask for crumbs. *(puts hand into pocket to hunt for crumbs and turns it out)* Are you hungry, too, poor Melchisedek? I'm very sorry, I haven't one crumb left. Go home, Melchisedek, and tell your wife that there was nothing in my pocket. She's not as hungry as I am.

(First rat off under bed)

Good night. Poor thing. *(crosses back to armchair, drops into chair, and takes Emily in her arms)* Do you hear, Emily, why don't you say something? Sometimes I'm sure you could, if you tried. You are the only relation I have in the world. Why don't you try? Do you hear? I've walked a thousand miles today, and they have done nothing but scold me from morning until night. And because I could not find that last thing the cook sent me for, they would not give me any supper. Some men laughed at me because my old shoes made me slip down in the mud. I'm covered with mud now. And they laughed.

(Wind)

(passionately) Do you hear? *(pauses and breaks out again)* You are nothing but a doll! You care for nothing. You are stuffed with sawdust. You never had a heart. Nothing could ever make you feel. You are a doll! *(throws Emily on stool and cries - then picks her up, sets her in chair; sits on stool, elbows on knees, and gazes at her relentingly)* You can't help being a doll, I suppose, any more than good-natured Ermengarde can help being stupid or Lavinia and Jessie can help not having any sense. We are not all made alike. I oughtn't have slapped you. You were born a doll - perhaps you do your sawdust best.

(knock on door)

I wonder who it is. *(rising hesitating)* Lottie is in bed and poor Becky was crying when I came through the kitchen. The cook was in a passion and she couldn't get away.

(SARA opens door, sees LOTTIE alarmed, surprised.

Enter LOTTIE in nightgown, hugging a birthday doll. Wind)

Oh, Lottie, you oughtn't to come here so late. Miss Minchin would be so cross if she caught you. What do you want, darling?

LOTTIE - *(who has run to SARA and is clinging to her)* I want you, Mamma Sara. Oh, I had such an ugly dream, and I got frightened.

SARA - *(leads her to armchair and takes her up in lap)* I'll hug you a minute, Lottie, but you mustn't stay - it's too cold.

LOTTIE - Hug me and kiss me like a real Mamma - Sara, it was such an ugly dream.

SARA - *(hugs her)* Are you better now, darling?

LOTTIE - Yes. You are such a comfy hugger, Sara. *(sits up cheerfully and sees doll on ottoman)* There's Emily. She's not so pretty as Lady Arabella, is she?

SARA - No, but she's the only relation I've got in the world. My Papa gave her to me when he brought me to Miss Minchin's four years ago.

LOTTIE - *(putting her doll beside Emily)* There, Emily, Lady Arabella has come to see you. *(to SARA)* Have you seen your rat lately, Mamma Sara?

SARA - Yes - poor Melchisedek - he came out tonight to beg for crumbs, and I hadn't any for him. But there, Lottie dear, you must not stay in the cold. *(coaxing her)* You won't have any more ugly dreams - for Sara will keep thinking good dreams for you after you've gone back to bye-lows. You must run back now, like a sweet Lottie.

LOTTIE - Oh, but Sara, I like to stay with you. I like your old garret and Emily and the rat.

(Wind and snow)

SARA - But listen to the wind. See the snow coming through the broken window. You mustn't stay here in your little nightie. I'll take you to the top of the stairs and you must go back to bed.

LOTTIE - But mayn't I say my seven times to you before I go? I have to say it to Miss Amelia in the morning. May I sit here on your bed *(does so)* and say it?

SARA - *(kneeling in front of LOTTIE)* Well, you can say it to me once.

LOTTIE - *(singsong)* Seven times one are seven -

Seven times two are fourteen -

Seven times three are twenty-one -

Seven times four are forty-eight -

SARA - *(gently)* Oh, no, Lottie, not forty-eight.

LOTTIE - *(anxiously)* Not forty-eight

SARA - *(suggestively)* Not forty-eight

LOTTIE - *(grasping at straws)* Not forty-eight - then - it's sumety other eight

SARA - *(encouragingly)* Seven times one are seven -

Seven times two are fourteen -

LOTTIE - *(dawning hope)* Seven times three are twenty-one -

(excited haste) Seven times four are twenty-eight -

SARA - *(hugs and kisses her)* Yes, that's it - go on.

LOTTIE - *(much cheered - singsong)* Seven times five are thirty-five –

Seven times six are forty-two -

Seven times seven are forty-nine -

Seven times eight are fifty-six -

(slowing up) seven times - nine - seven times - seven times - nine - seven times nine are –

(despairingly) Oh, Sara, seven times nine is such a hard one.

SARA - *(slow, suggestively)* Seven times nine - are - si - si -
Seven times nine are six -

LOTTIE - *(catching her up with a shout of glee)* Sixty-three - seven times nine are sixty-three –

(rattles off with triumphant glee and ease) Seven times ten are seventy -

Seven times eleven are seventy-seven and seven times twelve are eighty-four.

SARA - *(hugs her)* That's beautiful - all you have to remember is seven fours are twenty-eight and seven nines are sixty-three. Now we must go, pet.

(SARA sets LOTTIE down - giving her doll - leads her out of room door, exiting.

Moments pass before ERMENGARDE enters, a pile of books under her arm.

She is dressed in nightgown, with bare feet, and has hair done in curl papers.)

ERMENGARDE - I wonder where's she's gone. I wonder if that nasty cook has sent her out in all the snow and slush. *(rises and sees hat and shawl on chair)* No, she's not gone out - there are her hat and shawl - they are dripping wet. It's a shame. *(puts books on table)*

(Wind)

(goes to bed) What a horrible little bed. She must nearly freeze to death on these cold nights. Oh, it is a shame. She's treated worse than poor little Becky, the scullery maid.

(Enter SARA)

Oh, Sara, you do look tired. You are quite pale.

SARA - I did not expect to see you tonight, Ermie.

ERMENGARDE - Miss Amelia has gone out to spend the night with her old aunt. No one else ever comes and looks into the bedrooms after we are in bed. I could stay here until morning if I wanted to. Oh, Sara, Papa has sent me some more books. *(dejectedly pointing to table and books on floor)* There they are.

SARA - *(delightedly)* Oh, has he? *(runs to books and sits on floor; looks at titles on books, opens them)* How beautiful! Carlyle's "French Revolution". I have so wanted to read that!

ERMENGARDE - I haven't. And Papa will be so cross if I don't. He'll want me to know all about it when I go home for the holidays. What shall I do?

SARA - *(excited)* Look here, Ermengarde. If you'll lend me these books, I'll read them and tell you everything that's in them afterwards, and I'll tell it so that you'll remember it too.

ERMENGARDE - Oh, goodness, Sara! Do you think you can?

SARA - I know I can. The little ones always remember what I tell them.

ERMENGARDE - *(pause)* Sara, if you'll do that, and make me remember, I'll-I'll give you anything.

SARA - I don't want you to give me anything, Ermie, I want your books. *(holds them tight in arms)* I want them!

ERMENGARDE - Take them then - you're welcome. I wish I wanted them - but I don't. I'm not clever, and my father is, and he thinks I ought to be.

SARA - What are you going to tell your father?

ERMENGARDE - Oh, he needn't know. He'll think I've read them.

SARA - *(putting books down and shaking her head slowly)* That's almost like telling lies and lies - well, you see, they are not only wicked - they're vulgar. Sometimes *(reflectively)* I've thought perhaps I might do something wicked - I might suddenly fly into a rage and kill Miss Minchin, you know, when she was ill-treating me - but I couldn't be vulgar. Why can't you tell your father I read them?

ERMENGARDE - He wants me to read them.

SARA - He wants you to know what is in them. And if I can tell it to you in an easy way and make you remember it, I should think he would like that.

ERMENGARDE - *(ruefully)* He'll like it if I learn anything in any way. You would if you were my father.

SARA - It's not your fault that -

ERMENGARDE - That what?

SARA - That you can't learn things quickly. If you can't, you can't. If I can - why, I can - that's all. Perhaps, to be able to learn things quickly isn't everything. To be kind is worth a great deal to other people. If Miss Minchin knew everything on earth and was like what she is now, she'd still be a detestable thing, and everybody would hate her. Lots of clever people have done harm and have been wicked. Look at -

(Rats squeak)

ERMENGARDE - *(gets on stool and screams)* Ah, rats! Are you not afraid of the rats, Sara?

SARA - *(on floor)* Not now. I was at first, but now they're a part of the story. There were always rats in prisons, and the prisoners tamed them with crumbs. That is how I tamed Melchisedek and his wife. *(calls rats)* Come on, Melchy dear, come, nice Melchy.

ERMENGARDE - *(stumbles)* Oh, don't call them out. Come back, Sara. Tell me some more stories - they are so nice.

(SARA and ERMENGARDE resume former positions)

SARA - Well, I tell myself stories about the people who live in the other houses in the square. The Large Family, you know.

ERMENGARDE - *(seated on stool)* Did Miss Minchin ever let you go there to tea?

SARA - *(shakes head)* No, she said visits were not suited to my station.

ERMENGARDE - Old cat!

SARA - But I watch them out of the garret window there. When I stand on the table under it, I can see all up and down the street. That's how I got to know the Lascar and the monkey.

ERMENGARDE - What Lascar and what monkey?

SARA - The Lascar is the Indian gentleman's servant and the monkey is the Indian gentleman's monkey.

ERMENGARDE - Where do they live?

SARA - They live next door. He is the rich gentleman who is always ill. *(stops and listens)* Did you hear something at the window?

ERMENGARDE - *(frightened)* Yes.

SARA - *(gets up and goes to window)* There's nothing there. *(laughs)* Perhaps Melchisedek and his wife are having a party under the roof. The Lascar lives in the next garret and the monkey lives with him - one day the monkey ran away and came in through my window, and the Lascar had to come after him.

ERMENGARDE - What, that Indian man in the white turban,

Sara? Did he really come in here?

SARA - Yes, and he took the monkey back. I like him and he likes me. I remember enough Hindustani to talk to him a little - so now he *salaams* to me when he sees me. Like this *(salaams – then stops and listens again)* I'm sure there's something at the window - it sounds like a cat trying to get in. *(goes to window)*

(ERMENGARDE stumbles)

(turns from window, pleased) Suppose, just suppose it was the monkey who got away again. Oh, I wish it was! *(tiptoes to window, lifts it and looks out)* It is the monkey! He has crept out of the Lascar's garret, and he saw the light.

ERMENGARDE - *(crossing to end of table)* Are you going to let him in, Sara?

SARA - *(on table)* Yes, it's too cold for monkeys to be out. They are delicate. I'll coax him in. He's quite close. How he shivers! He's so cold. He's quite tame. *(coaxingly)* Come along, monkey darling, I won't hurt you. *(takes monkey through window - jumps down and crosses to end of table and sits)*

ERMENGARDE - *(back of table)* Oh, Sara, how funny he is - aren't you afraid he'll bite you?

SARA - Oh, no. Nice monkey! Nice monkey! Oh, I do love little animal things.

ERMENGARDE - *(sits to right of table)* He looks like a very ugly baby.

SARA - *(laughs)* I beg your pardon, monkey, but I'm glad you are not a baby. Your mother couldn't be proud of you, and no one would dare to say you looked like any of your relations. Oh, I do like you! Perhaps he's sorry he's so ugly and it's always on his mind. I wonder if he has a mind. Monkey, my love, have you a mind?

ERMENGARDE - What are you going to do with him?

SARA - I shall let him sleep with me tonight, and then take him back to the Indian gentleman tomorrow. I am sorry to take you back, monkey, but you must go. You ought to be fondest of your own family and I'm not a real relation. But I am sorry. Oh, the company you would be to a person in a garret!

ERMENGARDE - Shall we take him back tonight?

SARA - It is too late tonight. I must keep you here, monkey, my love, but I'll be kind to you.

ERMENGARDE - Where will he sleep?

SARA - *(looks around)* Oh, I know - that cupboard. *(gets up, crosses to cupboard, and opens door)* See, I can make a bed for him here. I'll give him one of my pillows to lie on and cover him with my blanket. *(crosses to bed)*

ERMENGARDE - But you'll be so cold.

SARA - But I'm used to being cold and he isn't. I wasn't born in a tropical forest. Let's make his bed now and see if he likes it. *(takes pillow from bed)* You bring the blanket.

(ERMENGARDE takes blanket)

Yes, monkey, pet lamb, you shall have nice bye-lows and go rock-a-bye baby.

ERMENGARDE - What?

SARA - I mean rock-a-bye monkey *(makes bed in closet)* and Sara will take you back home to your family.

(Noise outside of BECKY coming upstairs)

ERMENGARDE - *(frightened)* What is that?

SARA - It is only Becky coming up to bed.

MINCHIN - *(outside door)* Rebecca, Rebecca!

SARA - *(fierce whisper)* Miss Minchin! She might come in!

(ERMENGARDE, looking wildly about the room, suddenly tucks nightgown around her and rolls under bed. SARA hurriedly shuts monkey up in cupboard.)

MINCHIN - *(outside)* You impudent, dishonest child! Cook tells me she has missed things repeatedly.

BECKY - *(sobbing)* 't warn't me, mum. I was 'ungry enough, but 't warn't me - never!

MINCHIN - You deserve to be sent to prison. Picking and stealing! Half a meat pie, indeed!

BECKY - 't warn't me. I could 'ave eat a whole un - but I never laid a finger on it.

MINCHIN - Don't tell falsehoods. Go to your room this instant!

(SARA standing, clenching her teeth, fisting her hands.

MISS MINCHIN heard outside, descending steps.)

SARA - The wicked, cruel thing! The cook takes things herself and then says Becky steals them. She doesn't! She doesn't! She's so hungry sometimes that she eats crusts out of the ash barrel!

ERMENGARDE - *(timidly)* Sara, are-are - I don't want to be rude, but - are you ever hungry?

SARA - *(passionately)* Yes, yes, I am. I'm so hungry now that I could almost eat you. And it makes it worse to hear poor Becky. She's hungrier than I am.

ERMENGARDE - *(gasps)* Oh, oh - and I never knew!

SARA - I didn't want you to know. It would have made me feel like a street beggar. I know I look like a street beggar.

ERMENGARDE - No, you don't! You don't! Your clothes are a little queer - but you couldn't look like a street beggar. You haven't a street-beggar face.

SARA - Only the other day, a little boy gave me a sixpence for charity - here it is. *(pulls out the thin ribbon from her neck)* He wouldn't have given me his Christmas sixpence if I hadn't looked as if I needed it.

(SARA and ERMENGARDE look at the sixpence and laugh a little)

ERMENGARDE - Who was he?

SARA - He was a darling little thing going to a party. He was one of the Large Family, the little one with the round legs - the one I call Guy Clarence. I suppose his nursery was crammed with Christmas presents and hampers full of cakes and things, and he could see I had nothing.

ERMENGARDE - *(suddenly)* Oh, Sara! What a silly thing I am not to have thought of it!

SARA - Of what?

ERMENGARDE - I've just thought of something splendid. I've just thought of something splendid!

SARA - What is it?

ERMENGARDE - *(excited)* This very afternoon, I had a box full of good things sent me. My aunt sent it. I haven't touched it. It's got cakes in it - and little meat pies and jam tarts and buns and redcurrant wine, and figs and raisins and chocolates. I'll creep back to my room and get it this minute. And we'll eat it now.

SARA - *(clutches ERMENGARDE'S arm)* Oh, it makes me faint to hear of it. You are good, Ermie. *(hug)* Do you think you could?

ERMENGARDE - I know I could.

SARA - Don't make a noise.

ERMENGARDE - *(runs to door, peeps out, then back to SARA)* The lights are out. Miss Minchin turned out the gas when she went down. Everybody is in bed. I can creep and creep, and no one will hear me. *(dance)*

SARA - Ermie, let's pretend - let's pretend it's a party - and oh, won't you invite the prisoner in the next cell?

ERMENGARDE - *(delighted)* Yes, yes! Let's knock on the wall now - the jailer won't hear.

SARA - *(goes to wall and knocks four times)* That means, 'Come to me through the secret passage under the wall, I have something to communicate.'

(SARA and ERMENGARDE listen until five knocks are heard in response)

She is coming.

(knock at door is heard, door opens and BECKY enters – she starts at sight of ERMENGARDE)

Don't be frightened, Becky. Miss Ermengarde is our friend - she's asked you to come in here, because she's going to bring a box of good things up here.

BECKY - To eat, miss? Things that's good to eat?

SARA - Yes, and we are going to pretend a party.

ERMENGARDE - And you shall have all you want to eat.

(All dance and exclaim. BECKY stops them by -)

BECKY - Shh! *(points down)*

ERMENGARDE - Oh, that old cat, Miss Minchin - but there's Magus and Brazil nuts and lots of good things.

BECKY - 'Ow 'eav'nly!

(ERMENGARDE drops shawl)

SARA - Ermie, you go for the box and we will set the table.

(SARA sends ERMENGARDE out of the door)

BECKY - Oh, miss! Oh, miss! I know it's you that asked her to let me come. It makes me cry to think of it.

SARA - *(cheerfully, embracing her)* No, no, you mustn't cry. We must make haste and set the table. What can we put on it? *(sees red shawl)* Here's her shawl - I know she won't mind. It will make such a nice red tablecloth.

(Picks it up and spreads it on table with BECKY'S help)

What next? Oh! *(clasps hands delightedly)* I know, I'll look for something in my old trunk - that I used to have when I was a princess. *(runs to trunk, opens it and rummages in it – stops and sees BECKY)* Becky, do you know what a banquet is?

BECKY - No, miss, is it something to be 'et, or something to be wore?

SARA - *(sitting by trunk)* It's a magnificent feast. Kings have them, and Queens, and Lord Mayors. We are going to have one. Now begin to pretend just as hard as ever you can - and straighten the richly embroidered tablecloth.

(SARA turns to trunk again, as BECKY straightens tablecloth. BECKY then stands, squeezing her eyes tight shut, clenching her hands and holding her breath. SARA takes package of handkerchiefs from trunk, rises to go to table, sees BECKY and laughs.)

SARA - What are you doing, Becky?

BECKY - *(opening her eyes and catching her breath)* I was

pretending, miss. It takes a good bit of strength.

SARA - Yes, it does - just at first. But it doesn't take so much when you get used to it. I'm used to it. Now what do you suppose these are?

BECKY - *(delighted)* They looks like 'ankerchiefs, miss, but I know they ain't.

SARA - No, they are not. They are plates and napkins – gold and silver plates and richly embroidered napkins - to match the tablecloth. These are the plates and these are the napkins.

(Giving each bundle to BECKY separately)

You must not take the napkins for the plates, or the plates for the napkins, Becky.

BECKY - Lor', no, miss. They ain't nothin' like each other.

SARA - No, they're not. If you pretend hard enough. *(steps back)* Don't they look nice?

BECKY - Jest lovely, miss. Particular them gold and silver plates.

SARA - Yes, but the embroidery on the napkins is beautiful. Nuns did it in a convent in Spain. *(suddenly)* Oh, Becky, I forgot to tell you. This isn't the Bastille now.

BECKY - *(eagerly)* Ain't it, miss? Lor' now, what has it turned into?

SARA - *(grandly)* It's a marble hall.

BECKY - A marble 'all? I say -

SARA - Yes, it's a marble hall in a palace - it's a banquet hall.

BECKY - *(looking around room, opening eyes wide)* A blanket 'all!

SARA - No - a banquet hall - that window opens into the vast conservatory where the tropical plants grow. *(suddenly)* Oh, that reminds me of flowers. We ought to have some flowers.

BECKY - Oh, yes, miss, we ought to have some flowers.

SARA - Where can we get flowers from? Oh, the trunk again. *(runs to trunk, tumbles out the contents; drags out old summer hat with flowers on it)* Here they are *(tears flowers off hat)* What shall we put them in? *(looks about and sees washstand)* Becky, there's something that looks like a toothbrush mug - but it isn't - it's a crystal flagon. Bring it here.

(BECKY brings it and SARA arranges flowers in it)

BECKY - There you are, miss. There's something else there, miss, that looks like a soapdish - but it ain't. Shall I get it?

SARA - *(nods)* Yes.

(BECKY brings it)

(takes it from BECKY) It's a gold epergne encrusted with gems. *(wreathes flowers about it)* Oh, Becky, Becky.

(Both gaze with delight; BECKY clutches her lips with one hand and lifts them up and down)

Now if we had something for bonbon dishes. There, I remember - I saw something this minute. The darling old trunk *(crosses to it)* it's like a fairy. *(takes out bundle of wool, wrapped in scarlet and white tissue paper; goes back of table, tears off paper and twists into shapes of little dishes.)*

BECKY - Ah, Miss Sara, this 'ere blanket 'all - I mean banket 'all, and all them golden gems - ain't them beautiful?

(SARA puts candle on table from mantel shelf. Enter ERMENGARDE with hamper of goodies - she starts back with exclamations of joy.)

ERMENGARDE - Oh, Sara, you are the cleverest girl I ever saw.

SARA - Isn't it nice? They are things out of my old trunk.

ERMENGARDE - And here's the hamper *(sets it on chair)*. You take the things out, Sara. You'll make them look nice.

BECKY - Yes, miss, you take them out - I don't dast trust myself.

SARA - Thank you. *(looks in box)* What a lovely cake. *(takes out same and puts it on table)* And mince pie - a chicken patty - and grapes - and oranges - and plum buns with sugar on - and crystallized fruit in an angel box and chocolate caramels.

BECKY - *(puts basket on bed, and chairs at table)* Chocolate camels *(arranging the goodies, etc., until table is quite decorated)*

ERMENGARDE - It's like a real party.

BECKY - It's like a Queen's table.

ERMENGARDE - *(suddenly)* I'll tell you what, Sara. Pretend you are a princess now and this is a royal feast.

SARA - But it's your feast. You must be the princess and we will be your maids of honour.

ERMENGARDE - Oh, I can't. I'm too fat, and I don't know how. You be her.

BECKY - Yes, miss - go on, you be her.

SARA - Well, if you want me to - *(pause, then suddenly)* but I've thought of something else. *(goes to fireplace)* Yes, there is a lot of paper and rubbish left in here. If we light it, it will blaze up for a few minutes, and we can pretend it's a real fire. By the time it stops blazing we shall forget it's not being real. *(strikes light on box, starts fire; the three girls before it)* Doesn't it look real? Now we will begin the party. *(from behind table)* Oh, girls!

This *(paper off a cake)* shall be my crown, and this my sceptre. *(making spill of paper)* Advance, fair damsels, and be seated at the banquet table. *(sings)* Tra-la-la ... Tra-la-la *(beats time with paper)* Take each other's hand and advance.

(BECKY not knowing how)

No, no. Ermie, show Becky how. *(sings again)* Tra-la-la

(BECKY and ERMENGARDE join hands and dance to music. BECKY falls over books.

Finally, at the end of strain, both are in chairs - all sit together)

My noble father, the King, who is absent on a long journey, has commanded me to feast you. *(addressing air)* What ho, there! Minstrels, strike up with your viols and your bassoons. Now -

(Door is thrown violently open - enter MISS MINCHIN. ERMENGARDE dives under table.

BECKY cowers with cake in hand. SARA stands behind table with crown on.)

MINCHIN - I have been suspecting something of this sort, but I did not dream of such audacity. Lavinia was telling the truth. *(to BECKY)* You audacious creature! You leave the house in the morning!

BECKY - Yes, 'm.

ERMENGARDE - Don't send her away, please. My aunt sent me the hamper. We're only having a party.

MINCHIN - *(witheringly)* So I see, with the Princess Sara at the head of the table. *(turns on SARA)* This is your doing, I know. Ermengarde would have never thought of such a thing. You decorated the table, I suppose, with this rubbish. *(to BECKY)* Go back to your garret!

(BECKY crosses, steals off, face in apron)

(to SARA) As for you, I will attend to you tomorrow. You shall have neither breakfast, dinner nor supper!

SARA - I've had neither dinner nor supper today, Miss Minchin.

MINCHIN - Then all the better. You will have something to remember. Don't stand there looking at me like that - *(SARA has not taken her eyes from MISS MINCHIN)* - put those things into the hamper again!

(to ERMENGARDE, after seeing her books on floor) Ermengarde, you have brought your beautiful new books into this dirty garret. Pick them up and go back to bed. You will stay there all tomorrow, and I shall write to your Papa. What would he say if he knew where you are tonight?

ERMENGARDE - I don't know, Miss Minchin.

MINCHIN - Take that hamper.

ERMENGARDE - Yes, Miss Minchin. *(does so, exits)*

(Noise heard of ERMENGARDE falling down stairs)

MINCHIN - *(turning on SARA fiercely)* What are you thinking of? Why do you stare at me in that fashion?

SARA - *(quietly)* I was wondering.

MINCHIN - What?

SARA - *(not pertly but sadly and quietly)* I was wondering what my Papa would say if he knew where I am tonight.

MINCHIN - *(threateningly)* You insolent, unmanageable child! How dare you! How dare you! I will leave you to wonder. Go to bed at once. *(exits)*

SARA - *(left alone, takes up Emily, sits on ottoman)* There isn't any party left, Emily - there isn't any princess - there's nothing left but the prisoner in the Bastille. *(head down and cries softly)* I won't cry. *(to table with Emily)* I'll go to bed and sleep. I can't pretend any more tonight. *(blows out candle)* I wish I could. *(going to bed)* I'll go to sleep and perhaps a dream will come to pretend for me. *(takes off shoes in bed)* I'll suppose a little to make it easier. Suppose there was a bright fire in that grate with lots of little dancing flames. Suppose there was a soft rug on the floor and that was a comfortable chair - and suppose the garret was furnished in lovely colours. *(voice becomes dreamy)* And suppose there was a little table by the fire with a little hot supper on it - and suppose this was a beautiful soft bed with white sheets and fleecy blankets and large downy pillows - suppose ... suppose ... *(falls asleep)*

(RAM DASS appears at window with JAMES. He carries one dark lantern. Surveys the room, sees SARA asleep, raises window, enters with others, and without noise makes the trick change, bringing everything through window. First, RAM DASS and JAMES clear away the old furniture. After furniture is cleared, Indian stuff is brought on and placed. At end of change three lamps are brought on. RAM DASS lays fire in grate and before lighting same stands with lighted taper in front of grate which is signal for JAMES to light his lamp. RAM DASS and JAMES then take books from tray on table, put them on cushions, and exit through window.)

(SARA wakes slowly, sees the wonderful change and is bewildered)

SARA - What a nice dream! I feel quite warm. *(stretches out arms, feels blanket dreamily)* I don't want to wake up. *(trying to sleep)* Oh, I am awakening. *(opens eyes, sees everything - thinks she is dreaming)* I have not wakened. I'm dreaming yet. *(looks around smiling, bewildered but waking)* It does not melt away - it stays. I never had such a dream before. *(pushes bedclothes aside, puts feet on floor, smiling)* I am dreaming, I'm getting out of bed. *(closes eyes as she gets out, as if to prolong dream; then opens eyes)* I'm dreaming, it stays real - I'm dreaming, it feels real. *(moves forward, staring about her)* It's bewitched, or I'm bewitched. *(words hurrying themselves)* I only think I see it all. But if I can only keep on thinking it, I don't care, I don't care!

(sudden outburst of emotion – sees fire and runs to it) A fire, a little supper. (kneels at fire - hands before it) A fire I only dreamed wouldn't be hot. *(jumping up, sees dressing gown and slippers)* A dressing gown! *(holding it to face, then putting it on)* It is real - it is, it must be. It's warm, it's soft. *(puts feet in slippers, cries out)* Slippers - they are real too. They are real, it's all real. I am not - I am not dreaming. *(sees books on cushions – runs to them)* Books, books! *(opens one, turns over leaves rapidly)* Someone has written something. Oh, what is it? *(runs to lamp – reads aloud)* "To the little girl in the garret, from a friend." *(clasping book to her breast, grabs up Emily and hugs her)* Oh, Emily! Oh, Papa! I don't know who it is, but somebody cares for me a little. I have a friend. Oh, Papa, I have a friend!

Curtain

END OF ACT II

ACT III

Mr Carrisford's study in house next door to 'Miss Minchin's Select Seminary for Young Ladies'. Room handsomely furnished. Window looks out on winter street. Chairs, bric-a-brac, cabinet, curtains, with soft cushions on window seat, lady's writing desk, fireplace with firedogs. A table with books on it, and a big armchair nearby. Oriental rugs on floor with a tiger's head rug for Donald. Large sofa beside baby grand piano. Noah's Ark with animals in it.

At the rise of curtain: door opens. Enter RAM DASS, followed by DONALD, MAZIE, NORA and JANET CARMICHAEL. RAM DASS stands upstage. DONALD with a whoop sits on tiger's head. MAZIE and NORA go to piano to play with toys in ark.

JANET - Please tell Mr Carrisford we can wait as long as he likes. We'll go away if he doesn't want us. We're only come to cheer him up a little.

RAM DASS - The *Sahib* will be glad. I go. *(exits)*

DONALD - I'll sit here on the tiger's head. Gee up - gee up - gee up! I'm on the tiger's head.

JANET - Now, Donald, you must remember. Mr Carrisford has been very ill, and when you come to cheer up a person who is ill, you don't cheer him up at the top of your voice.

DONALD - *(riding tiger's head)* Well, I can cheer him up better when I'm sitting on the tiger's head than I can on a chair. Gee up! *(falls off)*

JANET - You can sit there, if you'll be quiet. *(crosses and sits in chair)* Mr Carrisford is very anxious today. He is waiting for Papa to come back from Paris. Mamma said we might help pass the time for him - because he likes us when we're quiet. *(at piano with animals)* I'm going to be quiet.

MAZIE - So am I.

DONALD - *(riding tiger boisterously)* We'll all be as quiet as mice.

JANET - *(to him)* Mice don't make a noise like that.

DONALD - A whole lot of mice might. A thousand mice might.

JANET - *(severely)* I don't believe fifty thousand mice might. And we have to be as quiet as one mouse. I'm the oldest and I'm responsible.

(MAZIE gets down from the piano and pushes DONALD off tiger's head on to the floor.

DONALD retaliates by pushing MAZIE off, onto the floor.)

MAZIE - Oh, Donald, you are rough!

DONALD - You pushed me off, I pushed you off. *(sits on tiger again)*

JANET - *(arranges pillows)* Now, that will be ready for him when Ram Dass brings him in, poor thing. *(leans head on hands on table)* Oh dear, I wish Papa would come. I do hope he will say he has found the lost little girl.

DONALD - Yes.

NORA - Perhaps he will bring her back from Paris.

DONALD - I wish he would. She could tell us about when her Papa shot this tiger in India. Mr Carrisford said Captain Crewe shot it.

MAZIE - I want her to be found because I want to play with her.

NORA - I want her to be found because I'm sorry for her.

JANET - I'm sorry for her. Perhaps she's a poor little beggar in the streets. She has no father and no mother, and Mr Carrisford does not know where she is. He only thinks she was sent to a boarding school in Paris.

(DONALD throws animals into ark)

GIRLS - Oh! - Ah! - Donald!

NORA - Papa has been to ever so many schools to look for her.

MAZIE - But he could never find her.

JANET - But he went to Paris on Thursday because he heard of a school where there was a little girl whose Papa died in India. If he doesn't find her this time, he says he shall not know what to do.

(DONALD bangs the piano)

GIRLS - Oh! - Donald! - Donald!

NORA - Oh, I wish it was time for him to come. *(to window)* Perhaps she is cold and miserable somewhere. And all the while, Mr Carrisford wants her so much.

MAZIE - *(tearfully)* Perhaps she's out in the wet in bare feet and torn frock. It makes me want to cry.

DONALD - *(taking stage manfully)* I say, if Papa doesn't bring her back from Paris, let's all go and look for her, every one of us. Let's go to the park and stand at the gate, and every time we see a little girl let's ask her what her name is.

JANET - *(desperately)* We can't let her stay lost and be poor always when she ought to be so rich and live in such a beautiful house. I can't bear it.

(Door opens. Enter MR CARRISFORD and RAM DASS. They cross to armchair.)

GIRLS - *(when they see him)* Oh, Mr Carrisford! - There you are! - Oh, how do you do? *(running to him and leading him down)*

CARRISFORD - How do you do, my dears? It's very good of you to come and see me.

NORA - We like to come.

JANET - *(who fixes pillows for MR CARRISFORD)* Mamma said we might come and see you on our way from the party.

MAZIE - We wanted to show you our party frocks.

DONALD - We're not going to make a noise. *(blows whistle)*

CARRISFORD - Oh, dear me, let me see. How smart you all are. Let me look at you.

DONALD - *(struts, showing coat and pants)* Would you like to see the back? *(showing it)*

NORA - Mamma lent me her locket.

MAZIE - *(showing frock)* Mine is quite a new frock.

DONALD - I have four pockets. *(showing them)* one, two, three ... *(loses fourth - suddenly finds it)* Ah, four!

CARRISFORD - I have only two.

DONALD - Oh, ho, he has only two!

JANET - Do you think you are any better, Mr Carrisford?

CARRISFORD - I'm afraid not, Janet. I'm anxious and it isn't good for me. I shall be better if your Papa brings me good news. Ram Dass, you may go.

(Exit RAM DASS)

NORA - He won't be long now. When he comes from Paris, he always comes in the afternoon.

DONALD - I say, I'll go to the window and watch for the cab. Mazie, you come and watch too.

JANET - Mr Carrisford, do you think he will come back and say he has found the lost little girl?

CARRISFORD - I hope so, Janet, I hope so. I shall be very unhappy if he does not.

NORA - Do you think that perhaps she is so poor that she is begging in the streets this very minute, while we are waiting for her to be found?

CARRISFORD - *(startled and miserable)* I hope not. I hope not. Heaven knows what she may be doing. That is what makes me so miserable.

DONALD - *(shouts from window)* Here's a cab, here's a cab!

CHILDREN - Oh!

DONALD - I believe it's going to stop here.

(MR CARRISFORD rises and partly turns upstage. NORA and JANET rise)

Oh, no, it isn't, and there's only a fat old lady in it with a blue bonnet on.

(MR CARRISFORD sinks back into chair)

JANET - Oh, Donald, you must be careful.

DONALD - I was careful. It was a cab. The cabman looked at this house when the umbrella was poked out.

CARRISFORD - *(pats JANET'S hand)* You are a nice little girl, Janet. Thank you.

JANET - *(kneels beside him)* I wish I could cheer you up until Papa does come - but when anyone feels ill perhaps cheering up is too loud.

CARRISFORD - Oh, no, no.

JANET - May we talk about the little girl?

CARRISFORD - I don't think I can talk about anything else just now.

NORA - We like her so much. We call her the little un-fairy princess.

CARRISFORD - Do you? Why?

JANET - It is because, though she is not exactly a fairy, she will be so rich when she is found that she will be like a princess in a fairy tale. We called her the fairy princess at first, but it didn't quite suit.

NORA - Is it true that her Papa gave all his money to a friend to put in a mine that had diamonds in it, and then the friend thought he had lost it all and ran away because he felt as if he was a robber?

JANET - *(hastily)* But he wasn't really, you know!

CARRISFORD - No, he wasn't really. The mine turned out well after all. But it was too late. Captain Crewe was dead. If he had lived he and his little girl would have been very rich indeed.

JANET - I'm sorry for the friend.

CARRISFORD - Are you?

JANET - I can't help it. He didn't mean to do it, and it would break his heart. I am sure it would break his heart.

CARRISFORD - You are an understanding little woman, Janet.

DONALD - *(from window, dancing up and down in seat with MAZIE)* There's a cab! It's stopping before the door. It is Papa!

CHILDREN - Oh! - Ah!

CARRISFORD - *(trying to rise)* I wish I could get up, but it's no use, I cannot, I cannot.

(NORA and JANET to window)

JANET - *(coming down)* Yes, it's Papa, but there is no little girl.

(Enter RAM DASS)

RAM DASS - *Sahib*, Mr Carmichael is at the door.

CARRISFORD - *(attempts to stand)* It is no use. What a wreck I am!

CHILDREN - May we go?

CARRISFORD - Yes, yes. Go, go.

(CHILDREN exit running, followed by RAM DASS)

MR CARMICHAEL - *(outside)* No, no, children. Not now.

CHILDREN - Daddy, daddy!

MR CARMICHAEL - Not now. You can come in after I have talked with Mr Carrisford. Go away and play with Ram Dass.

CHILDREN - All right.

(Enter MR CARMICHAEL)

CARRISFORD - *(shaking hands)* I am glad to see you - very glad. Pray sit down. What news do you bring?

MR CARMICHAEL - *(sits)* No good news, I am sorry to say. I went to the school in Paris and saw the little girl. But she is not the child you are searching for.

CARRISFORD - Then the search must begin all over again.

MR CARMICHAEL - I'm afraid so.

CARRISFORD - Have you any new suggestions to make?

MR CARMICHAEL - Well, perhaps. Are you quite sure the child was put in a school in Paris?

CARRISFORD - My dear fellow, I am sure of nothing.

MR CARMICHAEL - But you thought the school was in Paris?

CARRISFORD - Because her mother was a French woman and had wished that the child should be educated in Paris. It seemed only likely that she should be there.

MR CARMICHAEL - I assure you I have searched the schools in Paris thoroughly. The journey I have just returned from was really my last hope.

CARRISFORD - Carmichael, I must find her. I shall never get well until I do find her and give her the fortune the mine has made. It is hers, and she, poor child, may be begging in the streets. Poor Crewe put into the scheme every penny he owned, and he died thinking I had ruined him.

MR CARMICHAEL - You were not yourself at the time. You were stricken with brain fever two days after you left the place - remember that.

CARRISFORD - Yes, and when I returned to consciousness, poor Crewe was dead.

MR CARMICHAEL - You did not remember the child. You did not speak of her for weeks.

CARRISFORD - No, I had forgotten, and now I shall never remember.

MR CARMICHAEL - Come, come. We shall find her yet. *(rises)*

CARRISFORD - We will find her if we search every city in Europe. Help me to find her. *(shake hands)*

MR CARMICHAEL - We will find her. As you say - if she is alive she is somewhere. We have searched the schools in Paris. Let us try London.

CARRISFORD - There are schools enough in London. By the way, there is one next door.

MR CARMICHAEL - Then we will begin there. We cannot begin nearer than next door.

CARRISFORD - There's a child there who interests me, but she is not a pupil.

(Enter RAM DASS)

She is a little forlorn creature as unlike poor Crewe as a child could be. Well, Ram Dass?

RAM DASS - *Sahib*, the child, she herself has come - the child the *Sahib* felt pity for. She brings back the monkey who had again run away to her garret. I have asked that she remain. It was my thought that it would please the *Sahib* to see and speak with her.

MR CARMICHAEL - Who is she?

CARRISFORD - God knows. She is the child I spoke of - a little drudge at the school. *(to RAM DASS)* Yes, yes, I should like to see her. Go and bring her in. *(to Mr Carmichael)* While you have been away, I have been desperate. The days were so dark and long. Ram Dass told me of this child's miseries, and together we invented a romantic plan to help her. I suppose it was a childish thing to do, but it gave me something to plan and think of. Without the help of a Lascar like Ram Dass, however, it could not have been done.

(CHILDREN enter, except DONALD, crying and dancing with joy)

JANET - Mr Carrisford, Mr Carrisford! Papa, Papa! The little girl, she's the little girl we saw at the school!

MR CARMICHAEL / CARRISFORD - At the school?

NORA - She was quite a rich little girl in a beautiful frock.

MAZIE - And now she's poor and thin and ragged - at least almost ragged.

(Enter MRS CARMICHAEL)

MRS CARMICHAEL - My dears, my dears, what are you talking about all at once?

JANET - It's the little girl who made up names about us - and now she's quite poor and shabby.

MAZIE - She brought the monkey back.

DONALD - *(runs on, joining clamour)* I say, I say, she won't come in, she won't come in! I want her to come in! She talked Indian to Ram Dass, but she won't come in.

(during this DONALD jumps behind MR CARRISFORD, pulls his bathrobe and is taken away by MR CARMICHAEL)

CARRISFORD - *(to RAM DASS)* She spoke Hindustani?

RAM DASS - Yes, *Sahib*, a few words.

CARRISFORD - Ask her to come here.

(Exit RAM DASS)

MR CARMICHAEL - *(to MR CARRISFORD)* You must compose yourself. Remember your weakness. The fact that the child knows a little Hindustani may mean nothing. Don't prepare yourself for another disappointment.

CARRISFORD - No, no.

MR CARMICHAEL - *(to DONALD)* Here, you young rascal.

(Enter SARA with monkey in arm)

MRS CARMICHAEL - I believe it is the same child, but I should not have known her.

SARA - Your monkey got away again. He came to my garret window and I took him in last night. I would have brought him back if it had not been so late. I knew you were ill and might not like to be disturbed.

CARRISFORD - That was very thoughtful of you.

SARA - Shall I give him to the Lascar?

CARRISFORD - How do you know he is a Lascar?

SARA - Oh, I know Lascars. I was born in India.

CARRISFORD - *(excited)* You were born in India, were you? *(holds out his hand)* Come here. *(to RAM DASS)* Ram Dass, take the monkey away.

(Exit RAM DASS with monkey)

(to SARA) Come. You live next door, do you not?

SARA - Yes, sir, I live at Miss Minchin's Seminary.

CARRISFORD - She keeps a boarding school. But you are not a pupil, are you?

SARA - I don't think I know exactly what I am.

CARRISFORD - Why not?

SARA - At first I was a pupil and a parlour-boarder, but now ...

CARRISFORD - You were a pupil! What are you now?

SARA - I sleep in the garret next to the scullery maid. I run errands for the cook - I do anything she tells me - and I teach the little ones their lessons.

MRS CARMICHAEL - *(to MR CARMICHAEL)* Poor little thing.

CARRISFORD - *(gestures to MR CARMICHAEL as if agitation was too much for him)* Question her, Carmichael. Question her - I cannot.

MR CARMICHAEL - What do you mean by "at first" my child?

SARA - *(turning to him)* When I was first taken there by Papa.

MR CARMICHAEL - Where is your father?

SARA - My Papa died. He lost all his money and there was none left for me. There was no one to take care of me or to pay Miss Minchin.

CARRISFORD - *(cries loudly)* Carmichael! Carmichael!

MR CARMICHAEL - *(whispers aside to MR CARRISFORD)* We must not frighten her. *(to SARA)* And so - you were sent up into the garret and made a little drudge? That's about it, isn't it?

SARA - There was no one to take care of me. There was no money. I belong to nobody.

CARRISFORD - *(breaking in)* How-how did your father lose his money?

SARA - He did not lose it himself. He had a friend he was very fond of - it was his friend who took his money. I don't know how. *(to MR CARMICHAEL)* I don't understand. *(to MR CARRISFORD)* He trusted his friend too much.

CARRISFORD - *(agitated)* But, the friend might not have meant to do harm. It might have happened through a mistake.

SARA - But the suffering was just as bad for my Papa. It killed him.

CARRISFORD - Carmichael! *(faints)*

(Confusion. MR CARMICHAEL goes to MR CARRISFORD. SARA

stands before them, bewildered. She picks up shawl and starts to go.)

SARA - I think I had better go.

CARRISFORD - *(recovering)* Please, stay. What was your father's name?

SARA - His name was Ralph Crewe.

CARRISFORD - Oh!

SARA - Captain Ralph Crewe. He died in India.

CARRISFORD - Carmichael, it is the child - the child!

SARA - *(looking from MR CARRISFORD to MR CARMICHAEL, trembling)* What does he mean? What child am I?

CARRISFORD - I was your father's friend - he loved me - he trusted me. If he had lived he would have known - but now ... *(sinks back)*

MRS CARMICHAEL - *(to SARA)* My dear little girl. My poor little girl!

(CHILDREN start to go to SARA. JANET stops them.)

SARA - *(to MRS CARMICHAEL)* Did he know my Papa? Was he the wicked friend? Oh, do tell me!

MRS CARMICHAEL - He was not wicked, my dear. He did not really lose your Papa's money - he only thought he had lost it. He was ill, and when he got well your poor Papa was dead, and he didn't know where to find you.

SARA - And I was at Miss Minchin's all the time. Just on the other side of the wall.

MRS CARMICHAEL - He believed you were in school in France and he was continually misled by false clues. When he saw you pass by, looking so sad and neglected, he did not dream that you were his friend's poor child but, because you were a little girl too, he was sorry for you, and wanted to make you happier. And he told Ram Dass to climb into your garret window and try to make you comfortable.

SARA - *(joyfully)* Did Ram Dass bring the things? Did he tell Ram Dass to do it? Did he make the dream that came true?

MRS CARMICHAEL - Yes, my dear - yes! He is kind and good, and was sorry for you.

SARA - *(going to MR CARRISFORD)* You sent the things to me - the beautiful things - the beautiful, beautiful things - *you* sent them?

CARRISFORD - Yes, poor, dear child, I did.

SARA - Then it is you who are my friend. *(kneels to MR CARRISFORD)* It is you who are my friend!

MR CARMICHAEL - *(aside to MRS CARMICHAEL)* The man will be himself again in three weeks - look at his face already.

JAMES - *(outside)* Pardon me, ma'am, but Mr Carrisford is not well enough to see visitors.

MINCHIN - *(partly off stage)* I am sorry to disturb Mr Carrisford *(enters door)* but I must see him at once. I have explanations to make. *(meeting MR CARMICHAEL)* I am Miss Minchin, the proprietress of the Young Ladies' Seminary next door.

CARRISFORD - So, you are Miss Minchin?

MINCHIN - I am, sir.

CARRISFORD - In that case you have arrived at the right time. My solicitor, Mr Carmichael, was just on the point of going to see you.

   (MR CARMICHAEL bowed slightly; MISS MINCHIN looks from

him to MR CARRISFORD in amazement)

MINCHIN - Your solicitor! I do not understand. I have come here as a matter of duty. I have just discovered that you have been intruded upon through the forwardness of one of my pupils - a charity pupil. I came to explain that she intruded without my knowledge. *(turns to SARA indignantly)* Go home at once. You shall be severely punished. Go home at once!

(SARA rises and starts to go)

CHILDREN - *(going to MR CARRISFORD)* Oh, please don't let her go!

CARRISFORD - No, no, she is not going.

CHILDREN - Ah! *(return to sofa)*

MINCHIN - Not going?

CARRISFORD - No, Miss Minchin, she is not going home - if you give your house that name. Her home for the future will be with me.

MINCHIN - With you! With *you*? What does that mean?

CARRISFORD - That she is done with you, ma'am - with you and her misery and her garret.

MINCHIN - I am dumbfounded. Such insults! *(to SARA)* This is your doing - come back to the school at once. *(starts forward as though to take SARA)*

MR CARMICHAEL - *(coming downstage)* That will not do, Miss Minchin.

MINCHIN - *(violently)* Not do! How dare you interfere! *(to MR CARRISFORD)* How dare *you*? She shall go back if I have to call in the police.

CARRISFORD - The lady is too violent for me, Carmichael.

Please explain to her.

MR CARMICHAEL - I am Mr Carrisford's lawyer, ma'am. Mr Carrisford was an intimate friend of the late Captain Crewe. The fortune which Captain Crewe supposed he had lost has been recovered, and is now in Mr Carrisford's hands.

MINCHIN - *(startled)* The fortune! Sara's fortune? *(turns and stares aghast at SARA)*

MR CARMICHAEL - It will be Sara's fortune. It is Sara's fortune now, in fact. Certain events have increased it enormously. The diamond mines have retrieved themselves.

MINCHIN - The diamond mines!

MR CARMICHAEL - The diamond mines. There are not many princesses, Miss Minchin, who are richer than your little charity pupil, Sara Crewe, will be. Mr Carrisford has been searching for her and he has found her at last, and he will keep her.

MINCHIN - He found her under my care. I have done everything for her. But for me she should have starved in the streets.

CARRISFORD - *(angrily)* As to starving in the streets, she might have starved more comfortably there than in your garret.

MINCHIN - *(to MR CARMICHAEL)* Captain Crewe left her in my charge. She must return to it until she is of age. She can be a parlour boarder again. She must finish her education. The law will interfere in my behalf.

MR CARMICHAEL - No, the law will not, Miss Minchin. Captain Crewe instituted Mr Carrisford her guardian long ago. If Sara wishes to return to you, I dare say he would not refuse her. But that rests with Sara.

MICHIN - Then I appeal to Sara. *(to SARA)* I have not spoiled you perhaps, but you know that your Papa was pleased with your progress. And ... ahem ... I have always been fond of you.

SARA - Have you, Miss Minchin? I did not know that.

MINCHIN - You ought to have known it, but children, unfortunately, never know what is best for them. Amelia and I always said you were the cleverest child in the school. Will you not do your duty to your poor Papa and come home with me?

SARA - *(steps forward)* I will not. *(speaks quietly, steadily, and politely, looking squarely at MISS MINCHIN)* You know why I will not go home with you, Miss Minchin. You know quite well.

MINCHIN - *(spitefully)* Then you will never see your little companions again. I will see that Ermengarde and Lottie are kept away -

MR CARMICHAEL - *(firmly polite)* Excuse me. She will see anyone she wishes to see. The parents of Miss Crewe's fellow-pupils are not likely to refuse her invitations to visit her at her guardian's house. Mr Carrisford will attend to that.

(MISS MINCHIN goes wrathfully to MR CARMICHAEL)

CARRISFORD - Ram Dass, show this lady out. That is all, Miss Minchin. Your bill will be paid.

MINCHIN - *(makes for MR CARRISFORD)* You have not undertaken an easy charge. You will discover that very soon. The child is neither truthful nor grateful. I suppose *(to SARA)* that you feel now that you are a princess again.

SARA - *(dignified)* I tried not to be anything else - even when I was coldest and hungriest.

MINCHIN - *(acidly)* Now it will not be necessary to try.

(MISS MINCHIN looks around and, putting shawl over her head, exits. RAM DASS follows her off. DONALD whistles.)

CHILDREN - *(delightfully)* Goodbye.

SARA - *(goes toward MR CARRISFORD, drawing in a breath; shuts eyes then opens them wide with wondering expression, like waking from dream of night before)* I-I did not wake up from the other - last night. That was real. I shall not wake from *this*, shall I?

CARRISFORD - No, no, you shall never wake up again to anything that is not happiness.

SARA - But there is another little girl - she is as lonely and cold and hungry as I was - *can* you save her too?

CARRISFORD - Yes, indeed. Who is she?

SARA - Her name is Becky – she is the scullery maid. She has no one but me, and she will miss me so. She was the prisoner in the next cell.

CHILDREN - *(rushing around her, joyfully)* You're found! We're so glad you're found!

SARA - I didn't know I was lost, and now I'm found and I can't quite believe it.

MRS CARMICHAEL - What shall we do to make her feel that her troubles are over and that she may be happy as she used to be?

DONALD - You said you would tell us a story. Tell us one now, Sara.

SARA - Shall I?

CHILDREN - Yes! - Oh, yes! - A story!

SARA - Just as I used to?

CHILDREN - Just as you used to.

SARA - Well - once upon a time ... long, long ago ... there lived a little princess ...

Curtain

END OF ACT III

RACHEL LOUISE LAWRENCE

British author who translates and adapts folklore and fairytales from original texts and puts them back into print.

Since writing her first story at the age of six, Rachel has never lost her love of writing and reading. A keen wildlife photographer and gardener, she is currently working on several writing projects.

Why not follow her?

/Rachel.Louise.Lawrence

@RLLawrenceBP

/RLLawrenceBP

/RachelLouiseLawrence

Or visit her website: **www.rachellouiselawrence.com**

Made in the USA
Lexington, KY
25 January 2018